SAYINGS

THAT

SAVED

MY

SANITY

Journey to Freedom

Foreword
by
Nathan Lee

James S. Woodroof

ISBN: 978-1-63452-127-7

STRUGGLES PUBLISHERS
107 North Sowell St.
Searcy, AR 72143

Cover design — Gino Greganti, Nashville, TN

Printed by Gospel Light Publishing Company, Delight, AR 71940

Scriptures (unless otherwise noted) are taken from The Holy Bible, *New International Version®* Copyright © 1973, 1978, 1984 by International Bible Society. Used by permission of Zondervan. All rights reserved.

Order from:

HARDING UNIVERSITY BOOKSTORE
915 E Market Ave.
Searcy, AR 72149
Phone: (501) 279-4700

or

THE BIBLE HOUSE
2207 West Beebe Capps
Searcy, AR 72143
Phone: (501) 268-9886

(To hear audio recordings of some of the material in this book, go to jimwoodroof.com)

Table of Contents

Testimonials

"After trying desperately to seek help with P.T.S.D. issues, I found **Coaching: Life Matters**, and met Terry Smith. He provided me with James Woodroof's book. I took the book home and tossed it on the table, unsure of how this was going to help the anger issues in my life. While having an episode of rage, I decided that I was out of options to help myself. I had tried medication, psychiatry, and mental health treatment at the VA hospital, only to find them unable to fix my problems. Faced with the possibility of being committed, I was out of options; so I picked up the book and read the introduction. I could not argue the fact that Jesus was one of the most "dominant figures" in recorded history, and a lovable being. I began to read with an open mind, and I learned a better way to live my own life. This book gave me something pure and positive to focus on. Practicing the sayings in this book literally changed my life. This book brought happiness back into my soul, and I will forever be grateful." (Gino Greganti)

"At the point in our lives in which my husband and I received this book, I found myself in a place where everything I had ever done to "fix it" was no longer working. This book was a wonderful tool to opening my mind, heart, and soul to a new perspective on life, love and people. The pages in this book along with Terry S. Smith and *Coaching: Life Matters* saved my husband, my marriage, and my life. I never knew this kind of happiness was possible for us." (Erin Greganti)

"After forty years of counseling, I find this book to be the best in making Jesus' teachings accessible to the everyday person."
(Dr. Terry Smith, President: Coaching: Life Matters.)

"Mr. Woodroof explains the Beatitudes in a way that makes them easy to understand. After reading 'The Pure in Heart' I realize I have been guilty of wearing a mask my whole life. I can tell the mask has been off a lot more lately. Reading this book has helped me get through my time of incarceration."
(Foster Sims, 2010-11 inmate of East Arkansas Dept. of Corrections).

"At a time in my life when I was very socially insecure, this book connected me with the message of Jesus in a way that generated a social and spiritual confidence within me that allowed me to move forward with my life. I am very grateful."
(Joe Walker, Ex-offender, State of Texas)

"I want to use this material in my jail classes, as I think it approaches life from a direction these inmates have never considered and gives new life and application to our culture. This is material that hits the heart at the center. I honestly think this book is needed; it concretizes the message of Jesus."
(Harold Scott, former missionary to New Zealand.)

Dedication

This book is dedicated to Horace M. Woodroof, a distant cousin born in Nashville, Tennessee in 1906, served a reformatory school sentence at fifteen and a five-year burglary sentence at twenty-five before killing a prison guard during an attempted prison break in 1931. Sentenced to death at that time, his sentence was later commuted to life imprisonment, and he spent 32 years in the Tennessee State Penitentiary (eleven of which were spent on death row). He evidently had lost his moral sanity.

Horace Woodroof could have spent those years in bitterness and rebellion. Instead, with only a fourth-grade education as background, Mr. Woodroof educated himself behind the prison walls and began teaching fellow inmates the technical skills of producing and repairing radios. He began a regular prison letter entitled "*The Inside Story*" which for years was ranked among the top ten such productions in the nation.

Mr. Woodroof later wrote a book entitled *Stone Wall College* in which he acknowledged his guilt but also described the prison conditions of that time: the food, the harsh inhuman treatment, the indignities, the hopelessness one feels at the sound of steel doors slamming shut, barring one from family, friends and the priceless freedom, peace and well-being humans inherently desire.

Tennessee Governor Frank Clement and his successor Governor Gordon Browning had become aware of the prison's inhumane conditions, but also of Woodroof's influence on his fellow inmates. During his incarceration Horace became an avid reader of books on electronics and physics and of the Bible which he read daily. This led eventually to his becoming a believer in Jesus. Years later, on December 27, 1962 Governor Buford Ellington ordered his release based on two factors: one, Horace's good behavior and, two, his poor health. Horace Woodroof was finally a free man.

But it was while still in prison that Horace became a "free man" — in both soul and spirit. He had found the path to freedom, though it was a long time coming. That same journey to freedom can be made by all who are literally in prisons of "stone walls," or the millions who are imprisoned in walls of hatred and greed, selfishness and guilt. Whatever may be the case, there is hope for recovery.

On the last page of his book Horace Woodroof writes: "It makes no difference who you are or where you are. The only thing that counts is your God-given mind and the thoughts engendered therein. I feel that if we can change our way of thinking—switch from negative to positive—then whatever ails us now will soon be cured. This is my final word and, while it is a borrowed philosophy, it comes straight from my heart."

It is my pleasure to dedicate this book to Horace M. Woodroof.

James S. Woodroof
(Sept. 9, 2014)

Preface

You may not be aware that you've lost—or are about to lose—your sanity (which may or may not be a sign you're on the verge). Or, you may be thinking your condition is just the way life is and, if so, "Life stinks." How desperate are you? How willing are you to look in unexpected places for possible answers? Or to take a second look in places you may already have written off, or to hear from people you might consider un-cool, politically incorrect or out-of-date? Is there a chance you might be missing the answer that's been right under your nose all along, but you were not aware of it? Could it be you've been looking for the answer in all the wrong places?

If you've read the above without losing your cool, closing the book and throwing it in the trash, you may very well be a candidate for complete wellness, full happiness, and total sanity. Are you willing to search for it?

In an NBC News report of 9/24/2009 there was an interesting news item:

JOBLESS MAN UNCOVERS GOLD HOARD WITH METAL DETECTOR

> An unemployed man has unearthed the largest hoard of Anglo-Saxon gold ever found with the help of his metal detector. Terry Harbert from Bumtwood, Staffordshire (England) stumbled on the hoard in a private field with his trusty 14-year old metal detector. Over five days in July (2009), the 55-year-old dug up a fortune on the farmland near his home. More than 1,500 pieces of treasure—including around 11 lbs of gold and 5.5 lbs of silver have been uncovered. Archeologists believe the hoard dates back to the seventh century and may have belonged to Saxon Royalty.

Does the above news report give you some hope? Are you willing to spend time and energy searching for what may be the 'largest hoard of happiness' you ever imagined existed?

Dr. Terry Smith, (Founder and President of *Coaching: Life Matters*) wrote:

> When I heard these teachings forty years ago I knew they were true. Growing up in brokenness, alcoholism, divorce,

depression and abandonment I was searching for something that made sense. The perspective given in this book illuminated a path that gave my wife and me the fundamental tools of how to love and be loved. On August 18, 2014 we celebrated our 49th anniversary. Practicing the relationship teaching contained in this book has opened our hearts to a path of joy that sits high above the circumstances of the trouble, heartache and injustice we all are familiar with in our world. I use this book as a practical tool in my own life and with those who seek counsel on how to live overcoming and joy-filled lives.

Originally this material was designed to include only the parables of Jesus under the title, *The Grace Stories of Jesus*. However, through the years many friends had requested I put my material on the Beatitudes into print. But since so many excellent books had been published on the Sermon on the Mount, I felt my work would be redundant. But, after further consideration, I decided to add yet another book on the teachings of Jesus and include the material on his Beatitudes. I named the first edition of that expanded work, *Famous Sayings of Jesus*, thus allowing for incorporating both the Beatitudes and the Grace Stories under one title. Both are now included in this revised edition: *Sayings That Saved My Sanity*.

Writing a book is like having a baby: there is conception, gestation and delivery. Then that baby, once it's born, takes on a life of its own. You can never know where it will go or what it will do along the way. Some will love your baby; others will not; and some will just ignore it. But the fact remains: there it is! You can't abort a book after it's published; we're past book burnings, aren't we?

But the birth process is even more stressful if you have twins—which is what this book is—two creations wrapped in one cover. They are related and perhaps even strangely Siamese, joined at the head and heart. Hopefully the two parts will beat with one life, and where goes the one so goes the other. If the reader is blessed by the one, the reader will be blessed by the other.

One additional chapter has been added to the Beatitudes and Parables. It stands outside the stated Beatitude/Parable framework but is such an essential part of Jesus' teachings it had to be incorporated. Actually it undergirds, serves as background and gives focus to all of Jesus' teachings. It looms so large it could be overlooked—much as one standing in a forest might fail to see the forest for the trees. In light of the original metaphor being used to describe the twins ("two creations wrapped in one cover"), the additional chapter could be considered the "cover" wrapping the twins. So Chapter 19, entitled "*The Unexpected*," is included as a vital part of *Sayings That Saved My Sanity*. Without it, these sayings of Jesus might be either admired or ignored; but with it, the whole of Jesus' teachings becomes central, crucial and inescapable. Jesus once described the kingdom of heaven as "*... like a treasure hidden in a field. When a man found it, he hid it again, then in his joy went away and sold all he had and bought that field..*"

The remainder of this book is written to show the path to that treasure. You may appear to others like that homeless man wandering around with an out-dated metal detector. But who cares!? You can laugh all the way to the bank with the priceless treasure you will have found for a full and meaningful life.

I hope and pray that you will find that treasure as you ponder these **Sayings That Saved My Sanity**.

JSW

Foreword

How did this book get its name?

My name is Nathan Lee. I am a songwriter and a musician. I sing in prisons. Six years ago I formed a non-profit organization called "Send Musicians To Prison." I travel to Correctional Facilities around the United States with my friends. A couple of years ago, while processing my own personal journey, I spent some time with a Life Coach named Dr. Terry S. Smith. In the course of our time together, Dr. Smith gave me a copy of the book in your hand, but under the original title: *Famous Sayings of Jesus*.

I was so impressed with the book I took it to Curt Campbell, director of "Men of Valor," a non-profit work dedicated to providing hope to prisoners in Nashville, at the CCA Metro Correctional Facility. He organized a class of 50 inmates to study the book in detail. The class studied one Beatitude per week. Each of the students was given a blank journal and told to write his response to that particular Beatitude. Each week all fifty responses were placed in a large envelope which I gave to songwriter friends in and around Nashville—one envelope to each friend with this request: "Take these journal entries and write a song based on the inmates' responses to the Beatitudes—using their words."

A few months later, we were allowed to arrange a concert to be conducted in the prison by these eight songwriters. The concert took place on the 17th of June, 2014. All in all, some 250 people were in attendance—from inmates, to staff, to friends of the songwriters. The 50 inmates had seats of honor in the front 3 rows. There, on the printed program—right on the front cover was the title: "The Beatitudes Through The Eyes and Hearts of The Incarcerated." Inside the program were the names of the inmates listed as co-writers. Their words had been turned into lyrics and songs by the songwriters.

It was a powerful evening ... an evening that pointed toward the cross, an evening that reminded us that we are not forgotten ... an evening that focused on healing and freedom.

After my time with these inmates, and after meeting Mr. Woodroof, the idea came about to change the title to *"Sayings that Saved my Sanity."* When Mr. Woodroof and Dr. Smith made the suggestion, I thought it was a brilliant idea.

I am deeply grateful that Mr. Woodroof took the time to write this book. Not only did it save my sanity, but it pointed me toward the truth of where my sanity actually comes from—the Bible, through a relationship with Jesus.

May this book be a blessing to you as it has for me and so many of the incarcerated.

Nathan Lee

To view the Nashville June 17, 2014

prison concert, go to:

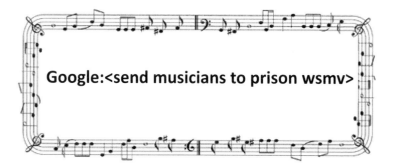

Google:<send musicians to prison wsmv>

Introduction

AFTER 2,000 YEARS, Jesus of Nazareth still remains the central figure of the human race—notwithstanding other religions, oriental as well as occidental—some older, some younger. Jesus still remains earth's most important human. H. G. Wells was asked by the *American Magazine* to write a story of six of earth's greatest men in the order of their prominence. He accepted the request and penned the article in which he, as an historian, gave his impression of Jesus of Nazareth. Among other favorable observations, he said:

> Jesus of Nazareth is easily the dominant figure in history... He left no impress on the historical record of his time. Yet more than nineteen hundred years later, a historian like myself who doesn't even call himself a Christian, finds the picture centering irresistibly around the life and character of this simple, lovable man.[1]

No doubt many factors have contributed to Jesus' lasting dominant influence, but one of the most prominent is his teachings. His contemporaries often were "amazed" at his teaching (Mt.7:28). "All spoke well of him and were amazed at the gracious words that came from his lips." (Lk.4:22) His captivating teachings began when he was a pre-teen at the temple in Jerusalem. "Everyone who heard him was amazed at his understanding and his answers." (Lk.2:47) Years later, the people of Capernaum were amazed at his teaching, because his message had authority. (Lk.4:32)

The crowds were also puzzled. The Jews were amazed and asked, "How did this man get such learning without having studied?" (Jn.7:15) Seemingly he had no qualifications, and this offended his hometown neighbors:

> Coming to his hometown, he began teaching the people in their synagogue, and they were amazed. ...Isn't this the carpenter's son? Isn't his mother's name Mary, and aren't his

---

[1] As quoted by N. B. Hardeman in the Dallas Lectures, (Dallas, TX, Eugene Smith Publisher, 1943), pp.122-125.

brothers James, Joseph, Simon and Judas? Aren't all his sisters with us? Where then did this man get all these things? And they took offense at him. (Mt.13:54-57)

My wife Louine and I once went to hear the Indianapolis symphony. As we sat waiting for the curtain to rise, I opened the printed program to see what the musical numbers were for the evening. Glancing through the program I came across a statement made by the conductor Mario Venzago: "You can't convince musicians with words. You have to convince them by your vision that must be so strong that they feel it and come to you."

His next statement startled me: "You can conduct without a baton, you can conduct without your hands, but you can't conduct without a strong vision."

I thought, "How similar that is to Isaiah's description of the Messiah;"

> He grew up before him like a tender shoot, and like a root out of dry ground. He had no beauty or majesty to attract us to him, nothing in his appearance that we should desire him. Like a man of suffering, and familiar with pain. Like one from whom people hide their faces he was despised, and we held him in low esteem. (Isa.53:2, 3)

Yet, Jesus was able to project a vision so strong it has resonated for 2,000 years and has drawn billions to him. He has done this, in a sense, "without a baton...without hands," i.e., without the qualifications which usually accompany such astonishing results. Jesus' "no baton...no hands" projection of his strong vision down through the ages has been captured in a well-known statement by James Allan Francis:

> Here is a man who was born in an obscure village, the child of a peasant woman. He grew up in another village. He worked in a carpenter shop until He was thirty. Then for three years He was an itinerant preacher. He never owned a home. He never wrote a book. He never held an office. He never had a family. He never went to college. He never put His foot inside a big city. He never traveled two hundred miles from the

place He was born. He never did one of the things that usually accompany greatness. He had no credentials but Himself.

While still a young man, the tide of popular opinion turned against him. His friends ran away. One of them denied Him. He was turned over to His enemies. He went through the mockery of a trial. He was nailed upon a cross between two thieves. While He was dying His executioners gambled for the only piece of property He had on earth—His coat. When He was dead, He was laid in a borrowed grave through the pity of a friend. Nineteen long centuries have come and gone, and today He is a centerpiece of the human race and leader of the column of progress.

I am far within the mark when I say that all the armies that ever marched, all the navies that were ever built, all the parliaments that ever sat, and all the kings that ever reigned, put together, have not affected the life of man upon this earth as powerfully as has that one solitary life. [2]

James Allan Francis

The presence of that one solitary life has changed the course of human history. His story is totally unique and for centuries has captivated the minds and hearts of those who "have ears to hear." I invite you to listen to his story.

---

[2] Adapted from a sermon by Dr. James Allan Frances in *The Real Jesus and Other Sermons*, titled "Arise Sir Knight" (Philadelphia: Judson Press, 1926), pp. 122-124.

PART ONE

The Beatitudes

Chapter 1

"Windows on the Beatitudes"

HOW did Jesus accomplish this captivation—without 'hands,' without physical force? And how has he continued to do it for 2,000 years? First, two negative observations must be made: 1) *Jesus did not come to introduce a shinier cage to keep us from doing what we really want to do.* The Ten Commandments of the Mosaic Law, to a large degree, had been designed to do that. Plus, the 613 oral prohibitions the Mishnah had placed around the Law stood as a hedge to make sure no one came even close to breaking the Law. But, as Paul confessed, sin took advantage of what was good and made it an instrument of death (Rom.7:7-12). What those who live under Law really *want* to do, they usually do, or they live as slaves under external restraint devoid of the joy of living freely from the heart.

Many people never rise above this 'slave' level of morality: they do what they should do only if someone in authority is standing over them making them do it, even though they don't want to. (We all can understand this in the context of strictly observing the highway speed limit. Even the best of us don't really want to go the exact speed limit—that is, unless a police officer nearby is watching us. Then we suddenly *want* to go the exact limit— until we're out of his sight. Then we push "resume!")

2) Similarly, a second thing Jesus did not come to do was to *make us do what we ought to do.* Yet,

It's easy to think "*I ought*" is the end,
The ultimate Christian ambition.
But, *ought* wears thin Sunday mornin' at ten
When you really *want* to go fishin'.

"*I should*" sounds good, but it's as dead as wood
When it comes to doin' what's right.
For what I *could*, what my head knows I *should*,
I usually don't in a tight.

If all our teachin' just has us reachin'
For that which I *should* or I *ought*,
I strongly surmise we've closed our eyes
To the real truth Jesus taught.

"*I want*" is the thing that gives life its zing,
And puts our money where our mouth is;
That gives us direction, provides our correction,
And keeps our feet where no doubt is.

So, when you *would* do a thing that you *should*,
But know from your past that you won't;
If you have faith as a grain, you'll find it's no pain,
To do what you *ought* if you *want*.

jsw (1970)

Jesus came to change our wants. At first this startles us because at the beginning of our Christian walk old habits keep raising their heads. They don't die easily. Someone observed, "Our bodies as living sacrifices keep crawling off the altar." But over time, with growing admiration of our Lord's glory, the transformation does take place:

> But we all with unveiled face beholding the glory of the Lord are being changed into his very likeness from one degree of glory to another. This comes from the Lord who is the Spirit. (2Cor.3:18, RSV)

This "from one degree of glory to another" implies that the changes in our lives occur over time, not always over night. That's encouraging. But something even more encouraging is that "This [transformation] comes from the Lord who is the Spirit." (3:18b)

This transformation delivers us from "boot strap" religion; we are being changed *by the Spirit*, not through human effort—but it *is* with human cooperation! God is not going to impose himself on an unwilling subject. The human will must willingly submit to the Divine will. Jesus said, "If anyone *chooses* to do God's will, he will know…" (Jn.7:17) Following Jesus has always been a matter of choice.

But, how does Jesus accomplish this transformation? First, it involves a principle that isn't even religious. It happens to non-religious people as well. It is the principle that "we become like what we love." There are no exceptions to this simple rule. Whether we acknowledge it or not, everyone becomes like what he worships. We become like our "god," big G or little.

Martin Luther said, "That in which your heart delights and on which your soul relies *is* your God." In a sense, we can choose our "god," but we cannot choose the consequences; that is settled—it's a done deal.

In another sense we are saved even from the choosing. Jesus said, "No one can come to me unless the Father who sent me draws him" (Jn.6:44). But, don't be discouraged thinking you may not be one of the "chosen." Just a breath before he made that statement he assured his hearers that it was his Father's will that everyone who looks to the Son and believes in him shall have eternal life (v.40). And then he makes a wonderful promise: "It is written in the prophets, 'They will all be taught by God.' Everyone who listens to the Father and learns from him comes to me." (6:45)

This brings us to the second principle of this transformation: *Jesus changes our wants by changing our thinking*. James Allen makes a disturbing but encouraging observation:

As You Think, You Travel

You are today where your thoughts have brought you;
You will be tomorrow where your thoughts take you…
You cannot escape the results of your thoughts.

You will realize the vision (not the idle wish) of your heart,
Be it base or beautiful, or a mixture of both...
For you will always gravitate towards that which you secretly most love...
In your hands will be placed the exact results of your thoughts;
You will receive what you earn; no more, no less...
Whatever your present environment may be, you will fall, remain,
Or rise with your thoughts, your wisdom, your ideal...
You will become as small as your controlling desire;
As great as your dominant aspiration.

So, in very practical terms, we are going to be what we think, and we're going to think what we see, read and hear. The subconscious confirms this. My subconscious often causes me to dream about what I read just before I fall asleep. Like computers. GIGO: "Garbage in, garbage out." But also "Good in, good out." What has most recently entered the mind before sleep often emerges in our dreams (an expression of the subconscious). "The good man brings good things out of the good stored up in him, and the evil man brings evil things out of the evil stored up in him." (Mt.12:35)

But, how can we know God's thinking? He lives in light unapproachable (ITim.6:16). Indeed he does, and no one is allowed to look on his face (Ex.33:20 and ITim.6:16). The scene at the giving of the Law of Moses—both sight and sound—was so terrifying that those who heard begged that no further word be spoken to them. "The sight was so terrifying that Moses said, 'I am trembling with fear.'" (Deut. 9:19, Heb.12:21) So, if we can't look on his face or bear to hear his earth-shaking voice, how can we know his will? That's a good question, and Jesus provided the answer: Jesus claimed that his teachings were not his but his Father's. "I do nothing on my own but speak just what the Father has taught me" (Jn.8:28). "So, whatever I say is just what the Father has told me to say." (12:50)

So, it is safe to conclude that Jesus serves us much like a prism serves light: he stands in between us and the "unapproachable light" and breaks down the light into its component parts so we mortals can receive it. Hence, when we listen to God's Son, we hear God's voice. 'Whatever he says is just what the Father has told him to say.' Christians put great store in this.

These thoughts may help us as we examine the Beatitudes which have been called "the essence of the essence" of Jesus' teaching. He is for believers the

Word of God in the flesh. As we begin the study of the Beatitudes and all that flows from them, we will be listening to his Father revealing the truths that transform us. "He who has ears had better listen." (The Net Bible)

Linguistically, the word "beatitude" has nothing to do with attitudes. The word *beatitude* comes from the Latin root 'beatus,' which means 'blessed.' Hence, because each of these eight sayings begins with "Blessed…," they are called the "Beatitudes." But practically speaking, the Beatitudes have everything to do with attitudes. Each of the eight 'blessed' sayings points up an attitude which characterizes the life of one truly following Jesus.

Following the analogy of Jesus being a prism breaking down the unapproachable light of God into essential, understandable components, I suggest humbly that the Beatitudes are the most concise and ready access to God's thinking available to the human mind. Flowing from that compact expression comes the remainder of the Sermon on the Mount as elaboration and explanation of those succinct statements. Then, the rest of the New Testament provides further elaboration and elucidation of the truths Jesus revealed. All the revealed will of God is rooted in Jesus as God's "prism," making his will known to a lost world. (This prism analogy is admittedly just a human attempt to give a possible key to understanding the process of revelation. Perhaps other perspectives will better help you grasp the eternal truths of God. I mention a few):

A simpler perspective pictures the Beatitudes as a lighthouse. Each beatitude serves as a stone resting on the one before or beneath it until the whole structure rises to the point of climax or completion: "You are the light of the world."

Another perspective or "window" is offered in the book **Walk This Way** by Tim Woodroof.[3] It pictures the Beatitudes as a mountain. Going up the mountain out of the world are the first four sayings which describe a believer coming *out* of the world to God: "Blessed are the poor in spirit," "Blessed are those who mourn," "Blessed are the meek," and reaching the pinnacle of the mountain: "Blessed are those who hunger and thirst after righteousness." Then, coming back down the mountain *into* the world are the last four Beatitudes representing the Christian's walk in the world:

---

[3] Tim Woodroof, *Walk This Way* (Colorado Springs: NavPress, 1999).

A fourth window allows the Beatitudes to be seen as a record of the birth and life of a believer in Christ. The first two sayings (the poor in spirit and the mourners) represent the repentance which a believer experiences. The "meek" is a word picture of the surrender of the penitent believer in baptism. Rising out of the water of baptism, much as a new born babe hungers for milk, the new-born Christian "hungers for righteousness." The final four qualities represent the believer's attitude and conduct in the world: mercy, purity of heart, peacemaking and being persecuted for righteousness. This, again, is a human attempt to communicate what we may have taken for granted or perhaps dismissed as beyond understanding.

A fifth window is a simple translation of the Beatitudes into Relationship Language. At the close of each chapter in Part One, that particular Beatitude will be translated into a verbal expression necessary for building, repairing and maintaining human relationships. These expressions are:

- "Blessed are the poor in spirit" translates: ***"I was wrong."***

- "Blessed are those who mourn" translates: ***"I'm sorry."***

- "Blessed are the meek" translates: ***"Let's do what's best for you."***

- "Blessed are those who hunger for righteousness" translates: ***"Let's do what's right, regardless."***

- "Blessed are the merciful" translates: ***"I forgive you."***

- "Blessed are the pure in heart" translates: ***"I love you only, and I trust you completely."***

- "Blessed are the peacemakers" translates: ***"Let me be first to make up."***

- "Blessed are those who are persecuted for righteousness" translates: ***"I'll make allowance for your bad day."***

Of all the windows through which we may see these eight simple but profound sayings, yet another is the clearest window of all: the one through which we see the Beatitudes as a *virtual biography of the man who spoke them*. The Beatitudes record his life here on earth: from his humble, human beginning in a manger to his agonizing death on a tree—we see him. He so mourned over sin—not his own, but ours—that he spent his life meekly foregoing his rights to fill our needs. He hungered and thirsted to do what was right and willingly spent himself forgiving others who failed. With purity of heart and undivided devotion he submitted himself to his Father's will. He came as the ultimate peacemaker giving his life for ours. And, rising triumphant over persecution and a cruel death, the kingdom literally became his (ICor. 15:20-28).

The first five windows we proposed may be dismissed if you so desire, but not this sixth one. The others might be distortions or may lack true clarity and perhaps should be taken even with a grain of salt, but not this one. In the Beatitudes we come face to face with Jesus of Nazareth.

Having made this observation, we turn now to consider each Beatitude individually, realizing we are making merely a human attempt to grasp ever so inadequately Him "who is, who was and who is to come."

Chapter 2

"The Poor in Spirit"

I WONDER what the people thought who first heard Jesus teach what we call the Beatitudes. It was probably similar to a question our youngest grandchild asked at the breakfast table one morning. Braden was probably five years old. I was explaining something to her. She listened intently for a few minutes and then turned to her grandmother and asked, "What's he talking about?" Can't you just imagine those people on that Galilean hillside, upon hearing Jesus announce, "Blessed are the poor in spirit," "Blessed are those who mourn," "Blessed are the meek," turned to the person beside them and asked: "What's he talking about?"

I imagine this was their response to many of Jesus' sayings, for he was always turning things upside down. 'To live you first must die,' 'to have you must give,' 'the first will be last, the last first,' 'love your enemies,' 'go the second mile,' 'turn the other cheek,' 'lend, expecting nothing in return.' If his sayings didn't anger his hearers, they at least must have confused them.

With this first Beatitude, "Blessed are the poor in spirit, for theirs is the kingdom of heaven," he says essentially: 'In order to go up, you first must go down.' On other occasions he told his self-seeking disciples, "If anyone wants to be first, he must be the very last, and the servant of all." (Mk. 9:35) Have you ever stepped onto an elevator, pushed the "UP" button, the door closed and, instead of going up, the elevator started down? Disorienting, isn't it? Someone on the elevator had pushed the "DOWN" button earlier. It almost causes vertigo. That's the effect this first Beatitude has on those who first hear it.

A young lady stepped into my office, sat down on the couch, eyes red from crying. She blurted out, "I'm so sick of me! I'm so tired of drinking, adulterating, carousing and cursing!" She continued, "I've been unfaithful to my husband while he's been overseas. I'm supposed to go join him in a few weeks, but I'm so ashamed to go like I am." I asked her, "How would you like to take your husband a brand-new wife?" She said, "What do you mean?" I said, "I mean you can take your husband a brand-new wife if you want to." Then, I asked her another question: "Did you know your picture is in the Bible?" Well, that really stumped her. "What are you talking about?" she asked.

I then gave her a Bible and asked her to turn to Matthew chapter 5 and read "Blessed are the poor in spirit..." and "Blessed are those who mourn." I said to her, "That's a picture of you. You came in here bawling like a dying calf in a hail storm, saying how sick of yourself you were, confessing your sins and hating yourself for being like that." At that she stopped crying—perhaps out of shock and curiosity. Shocked that I would use such a crude Middle Tennessee idiom to describe her mourning, and curious: "What in the world is this man going to say next?" I explained, "You have just walked through the first two doors that lead into the kingdom of God. You're experiencing repentance (poverty of spirit and mourning). If you act on this you can take your husband a brand-new wife. Her countenance changed immediately. She became aware that what was going on inside her was good. She was experiencing the first steps into God's reign in her life.

The usual spring meeting was in session at the College church that very week. This young lady came to hear the gospel preached. During that week at the invitation, down the aisle came this young woman. She confessed her faith and was immersed into Christ. She had brought her dead-to-sin body to be buried with Christ and to be raised to live a new life for which she would have no regrets.

I laugh when I remember what happened next. (This lady was one of the most uninhibited humans I'd ever met.) The morning after her baptism she burst into my office again—I think without even knocking—and stood with her hands on her hips and blurted out (seemingly her only level of communication), "Well, I've cleaned up the outside; now tell me how to clean up the inside!" She didn't realize her experience of abhorring her sinful life and surrendering herself meekly in baptism was already evidence of a cleaning going on inside her. I never heard from her again, but I trust she took her surprised husband a brand-new wife.

In the Beatitudes Jesus calls us to things not natural to fallen humanity. It's not natural to be humble, but to be proud. It's not natural to mourn over sin, but to *moan* over being caught. Nor is it natural for fallen humans to hunger and thirst to do right; our flesh urges us to get by with as much sinful activity as we can. It's not natural to be meek, but rather bullheaded. So, something must turn us around, and we don't like the idea of what that is. As we have noticed above, the first two Beatitudes describe it but, at the same time, hide a more severe name for it: Death! To be a follower of Jesus every believer must die to self.

Another young lady came to our home to talk. She was in despair. She wasn't crying; rather she was angry. She sat and poured out many years of pent up anger and resentment toward her husband. She concluded by saying, "It's just a vicious cycle; there's no way out." To which I replied, "No, there is a way out, but there's only one door out of the cycle of ill will and animosity you're experiencing. You're going to have to die to yourself." As far as I know, she never walked through that door. Dying to self is the most difficult step one ever makes, but it is absolutely necessary. Jesus said, "If anyone would come to me, he *must* deny himself, take up his cross and follow me." (Matt.16:24) Follow we may, but die we must. Oswald Chambers observed:

> The bedrock of Jesus Christ's kingdom is poverty, not possession; not decisions for Jesus Christ, but a sense of absolute futility—I cannot begin to do it. Then Jesus says—Blessed are you. That is the entrance, and it does take us a long while to believe we are poor! The knowledge of our own poverty brings us to the moral frontier where Jesus Christ works.[4]

Being a Christian is not primarily something you *do,* but something you *are,* or rather, *something you are becoming.* (Then, very decidedly, being a Christian is something you do because of who you are.) Chambers ob-

---

[4] Oswald Chambers, *My Utmost For His Highest* (New York, Dodd, Mead & Company, Inc, 1935), p.203.

served, "The only thing that exceeds right doing is right being. Jesus Christ came to put into any [person] who would let him a new heredity which would exceed the righteousness of the scribes and Pharisees."[5] During a seven year correspondence with an atheist I met in Norway, she made a humble, yearning admission which I'll never forget. She said, "All my life I have been a human *doing*. What I long for is to be a human *being*." But, when she saw the cost, she opted to remain a human doing.

The upward calling of which Jesus speaks calls our attention not to what we *are* but to an awareness of what we *are not*. "Blessed are the poor in spirit" is the first rung of the ladder leading to the higher calling—but it leads first downward to humility. This beatitude reaches down and touches us precisely where we are—where the Law of God leaves us—lost, undone sinners.

> There is no one righteous, not even one. There is no one who understands, no one who seeks God, all have turned away, they have together become worthless. There is no one who does good, not even one. (Rom.3:10-12)

Look at the Ten Commandments. Which of these have not we all broken? There's no denying it: We *are* spiritually impoverished. But this is not a cause for despair. In this first beatitude a blessing is placed precisely on our awareness of being nothing and having nothing. Jesus didn't say "Blessed are the blameless," but 'blessed are those who are aware of their sinfulness.' Until we are emptied of self we can never be filled with God. Christ is precious only to those who are aware of their poverty.

We noticed earlier that in the Bible there are pictures of people. There are two pictures in the Bible that relate to this beatitude. One picture is taken with a telephoto lens, zeroing in on people (individuals). It is the picture of a Pharisee and a tax collector who went up to the temple to pray. One was proud; the other was humble.

> Two men went up to the temple to pray, one a Pharisee and the other a tax collector. The Pharisee stood up and prayed about himself: "God, I thank you that I'm not like other

---

[5] Ibid., p.206.

men—robbers, evil doers, adulterers—or even like this tax collector. I fast twice a week and give a tenth of all I get."

But the tax collector stood at a distance. He would not even look up to heaven, but beat his breast and said, "God, be merciful to me, a sinner."

I tell you that this man, rather than the other, went home justified before God. For everyone who exalts himself will be humbled, and he who humbles himself will be exalted. (Luke 18:9-14)

The second picture was taken with a wide-angle lens which caught a whole group of people, a church no less, saying essentially the same thing as the Pharisee: The church at Laodicea is charged with saying: "I am rich, I have acquired wealth and do not need a thing."

Jesus replied,

But you do not realize that you are wretched, pitiful, poor, blind and naked. I counsel you to buy gold refined by fire, so you can become rich and white clothes to wear, so you can cover your shameful nakedness, and salve to put on your eyes, so you can see. (Rev. 3:15ff)

The startling realization is that my picture is in the Bible, and so is yours. The haunting question is, "Which one is a picture of me?" Am I like the proud Pharisee? Or am I like the humble tax collector? Pray it be the latter, for "Blessed are the poor in spirit, for theirs is the kingdom of heaven." (Mt. 5:3)

Jesus closed his sermon with this assurance: "Therefore, whoever hears these words of mine and puts them into practice is like a wise man who built his house on the rock"...etc (Mt.7:24). He was not giving instructions about building houses but building lives. So, his teachings were meant to be taken as principles for building successful lives. Thus, each of these sayings will be translated into "relationship language;" phrases or expressions we must use in building relationships not only with God but with other people.

The "Poor in spirit" Translated into Relationship Language:

How then does "Blessed are the poor in spirit..." translate into relationship language? Poverty of spirit, essentially, is humility. It is the opposite of pride. A basic, down-to-earth translation of poverty of spirit would be the ability to say, "**I was wrong.**" A prideful spirit says, "YOU were wrong." Being willing to admit wrong does not mean you always are wrong, but that you have the willingness to admit you are wrong; to say, "I've been wrong before; I could be wrong again."

Only those who are able to admit wrong are capable of building relationships that can weather the storms of life. When the 'rains come down and the streams rise and winds blow and beat against your life,' will your life stand? Only if you are able to say at times, "I was wrong."

Chapter 3

"The Mourners"

JESUS did not say, "Blessed are those who *moan*." To the ear this sounds something like what he said, but it's a long way from the heart of the second Beatitude. *Moaning* is not mourning. But we do moan! Do you realize how many things we moan about? The weather: it's either too hot or too cold; it's too wet or too dry. We moan about our health, our allergies or our rheumatism. With a closet full of clothes, we hear, "I don't have a thing to wear." Our job is either boring, too hard, or too many hours and too little pay. College students moan about campus food. Yes, you know what I'm going to say next: "You should have had to eat what we had to eat when I was in college!" We had no choice! Well, that's not completely true; we could choose to eat or not eat. Government surplus was our main source of food. And we had to eat our green beans very carefully; a big, fat, one-inch grub worm looked a lot like a green bean. And we moaned. But hey, here I am moaning about the food when I was in college. To all students, past and present: Get over it!! It's a sin. The children of Israel moaned about their food and died by the thousands, and Paul warns us not to follow their example. (ICor.10:10)

Not only do we moan; there is a long list of things we do to avoid *mourning*. Some of us "keep busy" so we don't have time to think about our brokenness. Others go on endless vacations. I've traveled a lot in my work, and I've seen many people who seem to think they will find contentment at the next stop, the next city, on the next cruise, or with the next wife. Others go on a spending spree: "Shop 'til I drop" is their motto. Millions turn to drink, drugs, food, or TV. Still others turn up the volume of MTV—anything to avoid silence. There's no end to the list of things we do to escape the discomfort of mourning. We'll even turn on others: blaming, judging and condemning others to avoid accepting responsibility for our own inappropriate words or actions.

Strange as it may seem, some turn even to religion thinking that will help, only to end up moaning about those new songs the youth like to sing. Those "Seven Eleven" songs: Seven words sung eleven times. Or we moan about the preacher—his sermons are too long or too short, too deep or too shallow. "We don't hear preaching like we used to hear." And so, we go on moaning instead of looking inside ourselves, and mourning, quietly mourning. It's in quietness and mourning that we find God and the comfort he promises.

Who would ever have thought that comfort would be found in mourning?! Or, in today's noise-filled culture, that peace would be found in quietness?!

IN SILENCE

In silence comes a loveliness; the dawn is ever still,
No noise accompanies the dew that glistens on the hill.
The sunrise comes up quietly,
The moon is never heard,
And love that animates the eye surpasses any word.
And prayer is best in solitude;
It seems so very odd, that long before, I did not know
In silence…
I'd find God.

Anonymous

A woman came down the aisle in tears. The preacher received her and let her mourn over her sins. A friend came up to comfort her. Thinking she was helping, she said, "Oh, dear, we all make mistakes." The preacher turned to the lady's friend and said calmly but sternly, "Go make us some coffee!" He later explained to the friend, "Mary was trying to die, and you wouldn't let her." We can become enablers, helping others avoid mourning. In our churches we need something I used to deride in other churches: the "mourner's bench." All churches need mourner's benches as do also our homes. When will we accept the fact that there is a blessing in mourning?!

> I walked a mile with Pleasure; She chatted all the way;
> But left me none the wiser for all she had to say.
> I walked a mile with Sorrow, And ne'er a word said she;
> But, oh! The things I learned from her, when Sorrow walked with me.

> —Robert Browning Hamilton

One example of the blessing of mourning stands out in my mind: King David of Israel (c.a. 1,000 BC). Unlike his son Solomon who seemed to lean toward moaning, David was a mourner. We all know David was a sinner. The good thing about David is that he also knew he was a sinner, and he mourned over it throughout most of his life. His psalms are filled with his mourning. But even David went to great lengths to avoid mourning—especially over his affair with Bathsheba (the granddaughter of his chief advisor Ahithophel). He committed adultery with another man's wife, impregnated her and then spent nine months trying to cover it up. He tried at first to implicate her husband Uriah. When that didn't work he had Uriah murdered and took Bathsheba to be his wife. During those long nine months of waiting for the birth of the child, David's health actually deteriorated. He tells of it in Ps.32:3-4:

> When I kept silent, my bones wasted away through my groaning all day long. For day and night your hand was heavy on me; my strength was sapped as in the heat of summer.

The devastation caused by unconfessed sin affected David's physical body. Only when Nathan the prophet cornered him (2Sam.12:1-4) did he break down and admit, "I have sinned!"

> Then I acknowledged my sin to you and did not cover up my iniquity. I said, "I will confess my transgressions to the LORD." And you forgave the guilt of my sin. (Ps.32:4)

Once confession of sin was made, deceit was expelled and health was restored.

21

Blessed is the one whose transgressions are forgiven, whose sins are covered. Blessed is the one whose sin the LORD does not count against them and in whose spirit is no deceit. (32:1, 2)

Once sin is exposed it loses its power; once sin is confessed the mourning brings comfort. Therefore, "Confess your sins to each other and pray for each other that you may be healed" (James 5:16). "Blessed are those who mourn, for they shall be comforted." That's a promise! Try it.

"Those who mourn" translated into Relationship Language:

"Poor in spirit," we have noted, translates "*I was wrong.*" But there is more than one way to say, "I was wrong." One way is to say, "O.K., so I was wrong; you've been wrong a thousand times!!" That is not what one says who is truly mourning, and one sure way to destroy a relationship is to display such an attitude. Then how does "Blessed are those who mourn" translate? Healthy mourning translates: "*I'm sorry.*" Admission of wrong plus remorse repairs damaged relationships. Stating "IF I have wronged you, I'm sorry" is also inadequate." Nor does "I'm sorry, BUT," and then proceed to justify yourself. I've done both and, probably, so have you. This only further alienates the offended and delays reconciliation. If you really want to build a relationship that will weather the storm, go ahead and say, "I'm sorry"—and mean it.

Chapter 4

"The Meek"

S TIFFNECKED and hard hearted" is what Jehovah called his chosen people. From the day he brought them out of Egypt till the Romans destroyed their holy city in A.D. 70 and beyond, this has been their nature. Like an obituary read at their funeral, 2 Chronicles 36:15, 16 laments:

> The Lord, the God of their forefathers, sent word to them through his messengers again and again, because he had pity on his people and on his dwelling place. But they mocked God's messengers, despised his words and scoffed at his prophets until the wrath of the Lord was aroused against his people, and there was no remedy.

This stubbornness was the very opposite of the quality to which Jesus called those who heard him speak those strange sayings on the hillside in Galilee. Probably to those people the call to meekness was the strangest of all.

It was spring time—the time of year the Romans had come to expect messianic uprisings among the Jews. And the region of Galilee was regularly the seedbed of those uprisings. Josephus observed, "These [Galileans] have an inviolable attachment to liberty, and they say God is their only Ruler and Lord" (Ant., XVIII, 1, 6:23). Salo Wittmayer Baron, in commenting on Josephus' description of the state of mind existing among the Galileans at the time of Jesus, says:

In this way arose the *Zealotic* faction, which for decades carried on a desperate guerilla warfare against the Romans. In its rationalization, the movement appeared as a special messianic belief that only through an armed uprising, sustained by God, could the enemy be expelled and God's reign of peace and universal prosperity dawn upon mankind. That is why an extremist wing among the "assassins" had no scruples about murdering a Roman official or a Jewish partisan of Rome. Galilee, with its numerous mountainous refuges, was the cradle and became the permanent home of the various groups constituting this bellicose sect.[6]

So, when Jesus came advocating meekness, they must have thought he had lost his mind. He went into detail, calling them to turn away from living by the law of retribution: "Eye for eye, tooth for tooth." (Mt.5:38) (They had misunderstood the Mosaic injunction as justification of retribution rather than a call for restraint from excessive punishment.)

And his elaboration must have further confused or angered them:

> Do not resist an evil person. If someone strikes you on the right cheek, turn to him the other also. And if someone wants to sue you and take your tunic, let him have your cloak as well. If someone forces you to go one mile, go with him two miles. (5:39)

He even dared to replace their age-old maxim with his new take on it:

> You have heard that it was said, 'Love your neighbor and hate your enemy.' But I tell you: 'Love your enemies and pray for those who persecute you that you may be sons of your Father in heaven.' (5:44, 45)

So, the call to meekness may well have been the strangest of his teachings for his hearers to understand and the most difficult for a writer to convey.

---

[6] Salo Wittmayer Baron, *A Social And Religious History of the Jews* (New York, Columbia Univ. Press, 1952), vol. II: Part II.

So, in this chapter we propose four *word pictures* of meekness to help us understand it. To introduce the first of these we must see what meekness is not: Contrary to what the 1st century Roman/Jewish world thought, *Meekness is not weakness.* It is actually *double strength.* Meekness is:

Power under control. In the 1954 movie *The Gladiator,* Victor Mature, playing the part of the slave Demetrius, graphically demonstrated meekness. The story went like this: His owners had become followers of the Way. They had been arrested and condemned for their new-found faith. The wife of Demetrius' master had been condemned to die in the Roman arena. She was tied to a post in the center of the arena; a bull was released for the purpose of goring her to death. Demetrius was placed in between the woman and the on-coming bull. Would Demetrius be able to protect his mistress or would both Demetrius and the woman die for the enjoyment of the spectators?

The bull came charging at his victims. Demetrius, a hulk of a man, grabbed the horns of the bull, twisted its neck until it broke! To this day I can still recall the sound of the bull's neck breaking as it gave way to the strength of Demetrius. The bull fell down dead. Demetrius then walked to the post, untied his mistress with great gentleness and carried her out of the arena. Even the bloodthirsty mob of spectators applauded him. Pagans had seen meekness in action. In Demetrius they had seen power, but they had seen also power under control. Even pagans appreciated what they saw and gave the intended victims the "thumbs up."

Forgoing my rights to fill another's need is another picture of meekness. It was the Fall of 1970. We had just returned to the U.S. from five-years in New Zealand. It was a beautiful Sunday morning. The Whitehaven church had been dismissed from the worship service, and our family had returned home for lunch. But that particular Sunday was a special day. It was the trial run of a new gasoline-powered model airplane our boys had made. Neither I nor they had ever had a gas-powered model. I sat in the bay window of our house in Memphis to watch the drama. After a preliminary start up, the boys filled the little gas tank, turned the propeller, the engine responded and the plane took off—straight up in the air. The boys were ecstatic! The maiden flight was a success. At least it started out that way.

Of course, when the plane ran out of gas, it took a nose dive to the ground. It hit the ground, broke both wings but not beyond repair. But there was an additional factor they had not considered: our two girls had invited an eight-year-old friend to eat lunch with us. She was learning to ride a bicycle. Of all the places on God's green earth that she could have been at that exact moment, she chose our front yard and that precise location. As the plane hit the ground, here she came precariously balancing the bike and ran right over the damaged plane and reduced it to match sticks!

The boys, seeing what was about to happen, were jumping up and down and running to the scene of the impending calamity. Our oldest son, who was a new convert, looked at the demolished plane and yelled at our guest, "You didn't have a right to run over our plane!" The little girl was shocked. She started crying and came into the house. She went to her room, packed her bag, went outside and started walking down the street to "who knows where." She just knew she wasn't welcome at our house.

I just sat still and watched to see what would develop. I saw the older son look down at his "rights" and then look at her and her need. He looked back at his "rights" and then again at her and her need. I could see the wheels turning in his head as these two points collided. I waited to see what he would do. Then, I saw his decision: he called out after her, "Wait," and he began running after her. I saw him put his arm on her shoulder and gently pat her. I couldn't hear what he said, but I imagine it ran something like this: "It's alright; it's just a plane. Come on back to our house." She wiped her nose with her sleeve and accompanied him back to the house. Everything was now alright: the hurt had been healed and the relationship had been restored. He had decided to forego his rights in order to fill her need. That's what this beatitude is talking about!

A third picture of meekness is **Serve rather than be served.** I saw this aspect of meekness demonstrated in Wal-Mart some years ago. I was in line at the Customer Service counter. Ahead of me was a lady with a dress in her hand. The Customer Service representative greeted her and said, "Do you wish to return the dress?" The customer replied, "Yes." But she was a bit fidgety, not completely comfortable with what she was doing. She said, "Well, actually I didn't buy the dress myself; a friend did." The Wal-Mart employee said, "Oh, that's O.K., we'll let you return it." That still didn't let the customer relax. She spoke again, "Uh, she actually didn't buy the dress at Wal-Mart." The employee then said, "That's alright; we'll buy it back from you." I knew Wal-Mart held the policy, "The customer is always right," but I had never seen it applied to that degree. Wal-Mart had decided to *'serve rather than be served.'* That's how meekness acts.

Don't get me wrong. That's how Wal-Mart treats its customers; that's not how they treat their competitors. Several years earlier I had stood outside their older store waiting for the doors to open at 8:00 a.m. I could see through the glass doors; the employees were having their regular daily "pep rally." There were six workers carrying a long box. The six workers were serving as pall bearers, and the box they were carrying was a coffin. Painted on the side of the coffin in large red letters was the name "K-Mart." They were in the process of burying K-Mart!

Wal-Mart is meek toward those who buy their goods, toward those who pay the bills. "But," you may be thinking, "how can they make any money with that as their policy?" Think for a moment: Jesus said, "Blessed are the meek *for they shall inherit the earth.*" By making Jesus' policy of meekness their policy on marketing, they have already 'inherited' half the earth, and they're working on the other half (China) right now. Wal-Mart is the largest retail distributor in the entire world! Jesus knew that meekness was the door to the heart—in business or in whatever fields of endeavor you may be engaged. It works with your mate, your children, your neighbors and your customers.

One caveat must be considered: "What about police and nations and **war?**" Nations should aim for the high principle of justice but often must apply force to accomplish justice—as when the nations of the world united to oppose the satanical forces of Nazism or today's resistance to Islamic extremists. Rulers are God's ministers for maintaining order in a godless world, and they "do not bear the sword in vain." (Rom.13:1-5) But the higher principle of meekness must be employed in building a personal relationship with God and with others. Justice toward nations combined with meekness toward God and individuals will, indeed, cause those who so live to "inherit the earth."

Laying down our lives for others is a fourth picture and is the deepest level of meekness. In a sense, this is an umbrella principle which covers all the other qualities of meekness. "Greater love has no one than this, that he lay down his life for his friends" (Jn.15:13). This quality has always been admired as noble and praiseworthy. And today the free world forever owes gratitude to the millions who have died in service to their country—laying down their lives for their fellow countrymen.

Pat Tillman, a 27 year-old athlete with the Arizona Cardinals is an example of this. After 911 he forfeited his $3.6 million position with the Cardinals to serve his country. His educational background qualified him to enter the services as an officer, but he chose to enlist as a private. He fought and died in the line of duty (ironically by 'friendly fire'), laying down his life for his friends. Stories could be multiplied of those who threw themselves on handgrenades or who did other selfless acts of bravery to save the lives of their friends. Who can ever forget those brave firemen who ran up the stairs of the Twin Towers to save those trapped in the burning buildings and in so doing laid down their lives? We owe them our eternal gratitude.

The ultimate picture of meekness, of course, is Jesus. Isaiah captured this picture as he foresaw the Suffering Servant lay down his life for others:

> He was despised and rejected by mankind,
> a man of suffering, and familiar with pain.
> Like one from whom people hide their faces
> he was despised, and we held him in low esteem.
>
> Surely he took up our pain
> and bore our suffering,
> yet we considered him punished by God,
> stricken by him, and afflicted.
>
> But he was pierced for our transgressions,
> he was crushed for our iniquities;
> the punishment that brought us peace was on him,
> and by his wounds we are healed.
>
> We all, like sheep, have gone astray,
> each of us has turned to our own way;
> and the LORD has laid on him
> the iniquity of us all.
>
> He was oppressed and afflicted,
> yet he did not open his mouth;

he was led like a lamb to the slaughter,
and as a sheep before its shearers is silent,
so he did not open his mouth.

By oppression and judgment he was taken away.
Yet who of his generation protested?
For he was cut off from the land of the living;
for the transgression of my people he was punished.

Isa. 53:3-7

Isaiah's prophecy described the meekness of the Messiah. Then watch Jesus fulfill that prophecy to the very nth degree. First, we notice meekness in Jesus when he was twelve years old. Having accompanied his parents to Jerusalem for the Passover, he got separated from them and stayed behind in Jerusalem (Lk.2:43-50). After searching for him among their relatives and friends, Joseph and Mary returned to the city and found Jesus sitting in the temple among the teachers, listening to them and asking them questions. Seemingly exasperated, his mother asked him, "Why have you treated us like this?" He answered, "Why were you looking for me? Didn't you know I had to be in my father's house?"

What follows that statement is truly amazing. Immediately after Jesus' answer, the record says, "They didn't understand what he was saying to them." But Luke observed: "Then [Jesus] went down to Nazareth with them and was obedient to them." Here was a teenager obedient to parents who did not understand him! That was meekness personified!

Again, when Jesus was thirty he submitted to baptism—another demonstration of meekness. John would have prevented him, but he wouldn't be dissuaded. In meekness he began his ministry, and he spent the rest of his earthly life serving others rather than being served. One of the most astonishing demonstrations of this was this stooping to wash his disciples' feet (Jn.13:2-8). He, their lord and master doing the work of a lowly slave! His final demonstration of meekness was his surrender to his father's will: he walked resolutely to the cross to lay down his life for even the enemies who killed him. And his call rings out to all who have ears to hear:

> Come to me, all you who are weary and burdened, and I will give you rest. Take my yoke upon you and learn from me, for I am meek and humble in heart, and you will find rest

for your souls. For my yoke is easy and my burden is light.
(Mt.11:28-30, ASV)

"Blessed are the Meek" translated into Relationship Language:

He is the embodiment of one who had unlimited power but chose to keep it under control; one who chose to forego his rights to fill others' needs; who chose to serve rather than be served, and who laid down his life for others.

The only question which remains for us is: "Do I want to live that kind of life?" It's a choice we all have to make. Should you and I decide to live that kind of life, he has promised that we shall inherit the earth.

How does meekness translate in our relationships with other humans? There will always be differences of opinion, differences in methods, priorities and perspectives and the perpetual problem of needs vs. rights. If relationships are to succeed, one quality must be mixed into the muddles of life: meekness. There always will be others who have needs to be met. Meekness in relationships translates, **"Let's do what's best for you."** We all have what we consider our "rights." As difficult as it may be, another's need trumps our rights. The apostle Paul, reflecting upon the spirit of the meek Savior, calls those who follow Jesus to:

> Do nothing out of selfish ambition or vain conceit. Rather, in humility value others above yourselves, not looking to your own interests but each of you to the interests of the others. In your relationships with one another, have the same mindset as Christ Jesus: Who, being in very nature God, did not consider equality with God something to be used to his own advantage; rather, he made himself nothing by taking the very nature of a servant, being made in human likeness. And being found in appearance as a man, he humbled himself by becoming obedient to death—even death on a cross. (Phil.2:6-8)

Chapter 5

"The Hungry and Thirsty"

I HAD A DRUG PROBLEM

I had a drug problem when I was a young person.
I was drug to church on Sunday morning;
I was drug to church on Sunday night;
I was drug to church on Wednesday night;
I was drug to Sunday School;
I was drug to Vacation Bible School;
I also was drug to the woodshed when I disobeyed my parent
told a lie, brought home a bad report card or
didn't speak with respect.
Those drugs are still in my veins, and they affect my behavior
in everything I do, say and think.
They are stronger than cocaine, crack or heroin.

(Author unknown)

THIS "drug problem" isn't ideal, but it sure beats roaming the streets with a gang, filled with hate and ending up in jail…or dead. Not only is this drug problem in America not ideal, it is no longer even real. Rather, we are fulfilling Adolph Hitler's dream. He said he wanted to "raise up a generation of youth devoid of conscience." We are seeing that dream come true today…in America. Many in our land have ignored God in their homes, outlawed God in our schools, banished him from the public square, ridiculed him on television, desecrated him in art and blasphemed him in much of our music. We are becoming "devoid of conscience."

While countries like Russia, which once banned the Bible are now begging for teachers to come and instruct their students in the Bible, America, which was founded on biblical principles does not allow our students to be instructed in the Bible. As a nation we are now morally adrift, having severed ourselves from our biblical moorings and our moral foundation. We have a drug problem, but it's not the one quoted above. Our problem is just the opposite. We're being drug away from God. We are seeing a generation come of age that does not know right from wrong. How strange "Blessed are those who hunger and thirst for righteousness" must sound to America's modern ear. How far we have drifted! We no longer know right from wrong!

In view of the above, we could narrow our focus in this chapter to simply a call from Jesus for us to do what's right: "Blessed are those who hunger to do what's right." And that would be a giant step! But, if we address this beatitude at this level alone, we will do it and ourselves an injustice. No question that in this beatitude Jesus tells us there is a blessing in doing what's right. But the fact is: we don't have it in ourselves to do what's right. In *My Utmost For His Highest* Oswald Chambers says of all the Beatitudes,

> Beware of placing Our Lord as a Teacher first. If Jesus Christ is a Teacher only, then all He can do is to tantalize me by erecting a standard I cannot attain. What is the use of presenting me with an ideal I cannot possibly come near? I am happier without knowing it. What is the good of telling me to be what I never can be? (p.203)

If we leave it at just the level of "doing what's right," we will have missed what is at the heart of this beatitude: a passionate love for God—a "hungering and thirsting" for God. Since we have no righteousness of our own, our hungering and thirsting for righteousness must be a hungering and thirsting for God and his righteousness. Paul confessed to the Roman Christians: "I know that nothing good lives in me, that is, in my sinful nature"

(7:18). Once we disconnect doing right from the God who is the God of right, we have no knowledge of what is right or strength to do what is right. "All of us have become like one who is unclean, and all our righteous acts are like "filthy rags" is Isaiah's confession (64:6).

But, this is no reason for despair. We are informed in ICor.1:30 that Christ "has become our wisdom from God,—that is, our righteousness, holiness and redemption." Also, "God has made him who had no sin to be sin for us, so that in him we might become the righteousness of God." (2Cor.5:21) So, the righteousness within our reach is not *acquired* by our 'doing what is right' but *imputed* because of what Christ did for us.

T. S. Elliot reminds us that even our actions can be right but our motives wrong: "The last temptation is the greatest treason; to do the right thing for the wrong reason." What is the right reason for doing the right thing? I maintain that the right reason must be a right relationship with God. It is because we love God that we do what is right. The unsettling question for us to answer is: "Do I really love God?" "Have I ever really loved God?"

It is neither accidental nor inconsequential that this blessing coincides with the first of all the commandments of the Law: "You shall love the Lord your God with all your heart, with all your soul, with all your strength, and with all your mind." (Lk. 10:27, Lev. 19:18) Jesus endorsed this: "Do this and you will live." (10:28) In the final analysis, Israel's national failure was that they did not love God. How many prophets this loving God had sent to Israel! Yet they turned away time and again. Jesus diagnosed their problem: "I know that you do not have the love of God in your hearts." (Jn.4:42) Rather, "…they loved praise from men more than praise from God." (12:43)

No Hebrew prophet more graphically portrays this unrequited love than does Hosea. After Hosea's wife Gomer had left him for other men, prostituting herself shamelessly, Hosea found her on an auction block being offered to the highest bidder. That's how far she had sunk in her immorality. God then instructed Hosea to buy her back. God went to this startling extreme to portray his love for Israel even in her fallen, depraved state (Hosea 3:1-3).

> The LORD said to me, "Go, show your love to your wife again, though she is loved by another and is an adulteress.

Love her as the LORD loves the Israelites, though they turn
to other gods and love the sacred raisin cakes."

So I bought her for fifteen shekels of silver and about a hom-
er and a lethek of barley. Then I told her, "You are to live
with me many days; you must not be a prostitute or be intimate with any man, and I will live with you."

This text in Hosea implies that Gomer was brought back as a slave and
required to live with Hosea against her will. She wasn't with Hosea because
she loved him but because she had to. Her relationship with Hosea was one
of a slave to her master. So it was between Israel and Jehovah.

Nostalgically, God remembered the early days of the nation and how he had
treated her with kindness and love as a father would treat a son (11:1-4):

> When Israel was a child, I loved him,
> and out of Egypt I called my son.
> But the more I called Israel,
> the further they went from me.
> They sacrificed to the Baals
> and they burned incense to images.
> It was I who taught Ephraim to walk,
> taking them by the arms;
> but they did not realize
> it was I who healed them.
> I led them with cords of human kindness,
> with ties of love;
> I lifted the yoke from their neck
> and bent down to feed them.

Though loving God is the most important commandment of the Law, we
see from Gomer's forced relationship with Hosea that love cannot be commanded any more than can hunger or thirst for righteousness be commanded. A relationship must be established out of respect and admiration
of God which draws us to him. We must be "attracted" to God.

How then is this relationship established? Beyond being "drug" to God,
there are two possibilities: 1) Some are *driven* to God out of desperation.
There are circumstances which drive people to God. It is true "there are no

atheists in foxholes." The failing of health, the approaching of death, the prospect of hell, and other impending crises have turned many to God. Though certainly not ideal motivations, they may serve as temporary goads to bring us to the reality of God and our responsibility to him.

2) The second possibility is being *drawn* to God. The ideal motivation is love—being drawn to God out of admiration of God. The psalmist knew this kind of motivation: "As a deer pants for streams of water, so my soul pants for you, O God. My soul thirsts for God, for the living God. When can I go and meet with God?" (Ps.42:1, 2) "Oh, how I love your law! I meditate on it all day long." (Ps.119:97) "How sweet are your words to my taste, sweeter than honey to my mouth." (v.103) "I will praise you, O Lord, with all my heart; I will tell of all your wonders." (Ps.9:1)

Saul of Tarsus, though at first "goaded" to God (Acts 9:5 KJV), grew to so love God that he longed for a deeper and deeper knowledge of him and considered such knowledge of greater value than all other possessions:

> Whatever was to my profit I now consider loss for the sake of Christ. What is more, I consider everything as loss compared to the surpassing greatness of knowing Christ Jesus my Lord, for whose sake I have lost all things. I consider them rubbish, that I may gain Christ and be found in him…I want to know Christ and the power of his resurrection and the fellowship of sharing in his suffering, becoming like him in his death, and so, somehow, to attain to the resurrection of the dead. (Phil.3:7-11)

C. S. Lewis had a similar Damascus road experience. Having spent most of his life fighting God, he finally gave in and became a loving proponent of God.

> …feeling the steady unrelenting approach of Him whom I desired so earnestly not to meet. That which I had greatly feared had at last come upon me. In the Trinity term of 1929 I gave in and admitted that God was God, and knelt and prayed: perhaps, that night, the most dejected and reluctant convert in all England.[7]

---

[7] C. S. Lewis, *Surprised By Joy* (London Geofrey Bles, 1955) pp.214,15.

So, beyond being drug to God, some are driven then eventually drawn to God. Being drawn is the ideal. Jesus said, "But I, when I am lifted up from the earth will draw all men to myself." (Jn.12:32) Only when we are drawn to Jesus will we truly follow him: "If you love me, you will obey what I command." (Jn.14:15)

I have been convinced for nearly a half a century that we come to God only through knowing Christ. This is what he said: "If you really knew me you would know my Father as well. From now on, you do know him and have seen him." (Jn.14:7) "Anyone who has seen me has seen the Father." (v.9) You can't love someone you don't know, and you can't know God to love him until you know Christ. And the more you know Christ, the more you'll know and love God. Hungering and thirsting for righteousness comes from being drawn to the foot of the cross and to the heart of God through Jesus.

When I was 23 years old I was assigned to speak at the Carolina Lectures on this very beatitude ("Those who hunger and thirst for righteousness"). I spoke on it, but I'm fairly positive those who heard the lecture knew not one thing more after the lecture than they did before. At the very best 'I had a firm grasp on the obvious.' I am convinced I was the only one affected by the lecture, and that was a negative effect. I felt I had attempted to "shoot a cannon ball through a pea shooter." For the first time in my young life I felt the magnitude of the Beatitudes—that one in particular, and it was more than I could handle—so much so that I didn't attempt to address the Beatitudes again for over ten years.

I was reintroduced to the Beatitudes in 1967. While in New Zealand I came across the classic book, *The Sermon on the Mount*, by D. Martin-Lloyd Jones. That book emboldened me to once again look into the Beatitudes, and I've been blessed ever since. Each of the Beatitudes contains an 'attitude' and also a corresponding blessing. The overall blessing is that, in them we see Christ who is our righteousness, and blessed are those who hunger and thirst after him, for they shall be filled.

As noted above, in relationship to God, hungering and thirsting for righteousness must be a hungering and thirsting for God himself. We have learned that "Christ is our righteousness." We have an *imputed* righteousness from God through Christ, not an *acquired* righteousness from our own efforts.

> **"Blessed are those who hunger and thirst for righteousness"**
> **translated into Relationship Language:**

However, in our relationships with others, we must define righteousness in a second biblical way, i.e., by right conduct toward God and toward one another. Jesus calls us to "Do to others as you would have them do to you" (Lk.6:31). But there may be times when others claim they have "needs" which are not in harmony with God's will. Without possessing some external code of ethics as a guide, one could be put in an untenable position. When emotions are involved, judgments can become cloudy and decisions uncertain. Some sensual male, for example, may plead with a virtuous female: "If you love me, you'll let me." What should she do? If she does love him, she may feel there is no right answer; that she's in a "Catch 22" and end up making the wrong decision. Without a moral point of reference outside her emotions, she's like a pilot flying without instruments or, if having them, doesn't know how to use them. When there is no visibility, the pilot must use and trust his instruments in order to come through the storm. When clouds of uncertainty move into relationships, one also must have an external point of reference. Defined in this way, "hungering and thirsting for righteousness" translates: *"Let's do what's right, regardless."*

But, that presses further the question: "What *is* right?" This question sounds much like the one Pilate asked Jesus (Jn.18:37). Jesus had just stated, "Everyone who is on the side of truth hears my voice." Pilate responded, rather dejectedly, "What is truth?" We also live in an age when many people don't know what is truth and what is right. In fact, many deny there is any truth and , consequently, that there is anything right or wrong.

Norman Geisler demonstrated this with his account of a young college student who submitted a paper denying there were any absolute moral principles.[8] The quality of the research and writing was exceptional—definitely an "A" paper. However, upon receiving the graded paper, the student saw written across the front: "F—I do not like blue folders." The student was

---

[8] Norman Geisler, "The Collapse of Modern Atheism," in Roy Abraham Varghese, ed., *The Intellectuals Speak Out About God.* (Regnery Gateway,Inc., 1984), p. 147.

incensed! He stormed into the professor's office protesting, "This is not fair! It's unjust! I should be graded on the content of my paper not on the color of the folder!"

The professor smiled and inquired, "Isn't this the paper that argued so forcefully that there are no such objective moral principles as justice and fairness? Did you not argue that everything is simply a matter of one's likes and dislikes?"

"Well, yes," the student replied.

"Then," said the professor, "I do not like blue folders. The grade is "F.""

The young man suddenly got the point. Although he had been unaware of it, he did in fact believe in the principles of justice and fairness. The lesson having been learned, the professor changed the grade to an "A."

Then we must ask another question: "Is the standard that which the majority wants?" Peer pressure would have us think so. And that might seem acceptable as long as we are in the majority. Once we become the minority, however, we see the injustice of such a standard. What the majority wants cannot be the standard of what is morally right or wrong.

Then, does might make right? If so, every bully (individual or corporate) becomes the standard of conduct for that culture—large or small.

Well, perhaps the government can determine what is right or wrong. Then we have another Hitler's Germany; another "Final Solution;" another Holocaust. As long as the issue is framed in such atrocious national actions as Hitler's, no thinking person would want such to be the standard.

But coming closer to home, "Does a mother have the right over the life of her unborn child?" The United States government ruling that she does have that right has resulted (since Roe vs. Wade in 1973 to the date of this writing) in the murdering of 53,310,843 unborn (or partially born) babies.

When the consequences of the above proposed standards are recognized, no healthy culture which chooses as its moral standard any of these shifting, sinking sands. We must ask, "Is there a fixed, timeless and universal ethic by which we may correctly judge what is right and what is wrong?"

The answer is: "yes." There *is* such a standard, held unconsciously though it may be. It became evident when the nations of the world assembled at Nuremburg, Germany after World War II to pass judgment on Hitler's Nazi regime. To my knowledge there was no debate prior to the trial to determine the standard of what was right or wrong. Of course, the procedural rules for conducting the trial were clearly stated, but even those rules were shaped by a prior universal awareness inherently sufficient within all humans to make just judgments. That international court examined the accused to determine whether or not they had violated that universally-accepted code of conduct. The Nazi perpetrators of those universally recognized wrongs were judged guilty of "crimes against humanity."

So there is a standard of "right and wrong." But who sets that standard? There is only one person history has proved to be that standard. He claimed to be that standard which, if followed, would lead to light, never to darkness (Jn. 8:12). He claimed to be the "way, the truth and the life" (14:6), and that whoever holds to his teachings holds to the truth, and that 'this truth would make him free' (8:32): Jesus of Nazareth.

Of course, a critic will charge, "But that's a matter of faith!" Precisely! And so is the acceptance of *any* would-be standard of morality. So, what is the solution? Simply this: Follow the standard that is the highest and noblest and which produces the ultimate good for humanity as a whole. Then, there's only one choice, only one person is the final standard. As one agnostic frankly admitted to me: "Of course, if I lived according to the Gospel's principles, I would be a better person; [and] if everybody did, the world would be a perfect world." What better proof of a universal standard could anyone want than that which "living according to the Gospel principles would produce a perfect world!" Jesus is that moral point of reference, and he alone can bring us safely through the storms of life.

Chapter 6

"The Merciful"

I T'S INTERESTING, but not surprising, that "Blessed are the merciful" should follow right on the heels of "those who hunger and thirst for righteousness," for sometimes those who are most hungry and thirsty for righteousness are also those least merciful to those who don't measure up to the supposed standard of righteousness. Without a proper understanding of righteousness, one is likely to fall into the trap of being judgmental. Later in his sermon, Jesus warned against judging others: "Do not judge, or you too will be judged. For in the same way you judge others, you will be judged, and with the measure you use, it will be measured to you" (Mt.7:1, 2). "What goes around comes around" is never more true than when we pronounce judgment on others. If you want mercy, show mercy!

Jesus went on to say (vv. 3-5) that judgment is improper because the sin in our own life disqualifies us to make proper judgment on the sins in the lives of others. We need to correct our own sins before we assume the right to correct others.

> Why do you look at the speck of sawdust in your brother's eye and pay no attention to the plank in your own eye? How can you say to your brother, 'Let me take the speck out of your eye,' when all the time there is a plank in your own eye? You hypocrite, first take the plank out of your own eye, and then you will see clearly to remove the speck from your brother's eye.

After the Pharisees condemned Jesus for allowing his disciples to eat grain on the Sabbath, Jesus replied, "If you had known what these words mean, 'I desire mercy, not sacrifice,' you would not have condemned the innocent." (Mt.12:7) On another occasion he instructed the Pharisees to "go and learn what this means: 'I desire mercy, not sacrifice.'" (9:13) He charged the Pharisees with "straining out gnats and swallowing camels" when he observed their meticulous tithing of mint, dill and cummin while neglecting the "weightier matters of the law—justice, mercy and faithfulness." (23:23, 24) Jesus' half-brother James concurred, urging us to "Speak and act like those who are going to be judged by the law that gives freedom, because judgment without mercy will be shown to anyone who has not been merciful. Mercy triumphs over judgment." (James 2:12, 13)

How many times we have seen this in our own experience! Some few years ago I was pulled over by the highway patrol. I was speeding. She asked to see my license. After looking it over, she handed it back to me and said with a smile: "Happy birthday." I had forgotten it was my birthday. The officer had shown me mercy instead of judgment. Nice birthday present!

I once spoke to a group of men in the federal penitentiary in Pennsylvania. How does an outsider address a group of criminals incarcerated for crimes ranging from armed robbery to murder? I began by saying, "You are here because you're receiving the just penalty for your actions." I then confessed that I was a fugitive from justice. I proceeded to tell them they weren't all that much different from those of us on the outside—except for the fact they were caught, and we were not. Are not all we outsiders, to one degree or other, fugitives from justice? Where would you be were it not for mercy?

I once witnessed something that would very much qualify as mercy. I attended my senior high school year as a dormie in a school away from home. I was involved in more than my share of foolish activities characteristic of teens. Thankfully, I was not involved in the following incident. A group of boys in the dorm were bowling...with coke bottles as the pins and a coke bottle as the ball. This idiotic game required setting up the "pins" at the end of the hall then proceed to the other end and "bowl" a coke bottle to see how many pins one could knock down. On that particular night when the bowler released his bottle an inquisitive student looked out his door at just that moment to see what all the noise was about. The bottle struck the student in the temple, killing him instantly. Needless to say, that incident brought an abrupt end to that sport, but it was too late to save the unfortunate victim.

How should the parents of that innocent student have reacted toward the bowler? Unintentional though it was, he had killed their only son. Here's what the bereaved parents did. They showed mercy to the guilty boy— they adopted him as their own son. You see, the boy who heaved the coke bottle was an orphan, and the couple had lost their son—their only son. When the offended decided to adopt the offender, mercy trumped both tragedies. The orphan received a home and the home received a son. Mercy triumphed over judgment.

The most astonishing recent example of forgiveness is the Amish family's treatment of the murderer of five young Amish girls. The headline of the October 5, 2006 *Times* in Nickel Mines, PA, read:

"Amish bury their girls and forgive killer and his family"

Journalist Tim Reid describes the almost surreal event:

> It began with a tiny horse-drawn hearse no more than a few feet long, its small, darkened windows almost entirely obscuring the simple pine coffin lying within.
>
> Inside lay Naomi Rose Ebersol, 7, her eyes closed, a white cap atop her head, her body covered by a white dress, her child's feet in white socks. All Amish women are buried in white: it symbolizes the purity of heaven.
>
> Behind her, 37 horse-drawn buggies joined the funeral procession, clip-clopping the mile down Mine Road from Naomi's house—and past the home of Charles Roberts, the gunman who killed her—to Georgetown Amish Cemetery, where she was buried at noon amid 100 family and friends.
>
> The men and women, wearing wide-brimmed, black hats and black bonnets, took one last look at Naomi, filing past the open coffin that has sat inside the Ebersol home for the past two days while her mother dressed her and her family touched her. Scores of cousins filled the home, bringing food and gazing at the little girl. Tears were shed and stories told. Then the coffin lid was sealed and the box lowered into its grave.

A year later Kate Naseef interviewed Steve Nolt, author of *Amish Grace: "How forgiveness transcended tragedy."* Naseef asked Nolt:

> Q: What did you learn about the Amish understanding and practice of forgiveness while you were writing this book? A: One of the main things I learned was how central forgiveness is to Amish theology and really to their whole values system. The Amish believe in a real sense that God's forgiveness of them is dependent on their extending forgiveness to other people. Their understanding of forgiveness is embedded in their culture and their history—their 500-year history that includes martyrs that did not seek revenge but asked for forgiveness for their persecutors. In one sense, this is part of their cultural DNA.
>
> Their understanding of forgiveness is that it is a long process, that it is difficult, that it is painful, that replacing bitter feelings toward someone is something that takes time, and they would say that happens only through God's grace. But they begin with expressing their intention to forgive, with the faith that the emotional forgiveness will follow over months and years. They don't begin with trying to blame someone or something.

Without question the Amish believe in showing mercy to their offenders, and their example will stand out forever in our memory.

But beyond forgiving others—which, admittedly is "a long process, difficult and painful" (Steve Nolt) —another sobering question takes us in a completely different yet paradoxically parallel direction: *Can we show mercy to ourselves?* At first glance this may seem outside the parameters of Jesus' teaching on mercy. Yet, when we recognize that Jesus considered 'loving our neighbor *as ourselves*' the second greatest commandment upon which hang all the law and the prophets (Mt.22:36-40), it becomes clear that showing mercy to ourselves is an integral part of the process of extending mercy to others. As Dan Eubanks observed, "Some should not love their neighbors as themselves because, if they did, they would destroy them."[9]

---

[9] Dan Eubanks, "Unresolved Guilt in the Church"- 1 (Austin, TX: Firm Foundation), Feb.8, 1997)

How prevalent in the church is self recrimination and failure to show mercy to ourselves? Batsell Barrett Baxter observed:

> I have been deeply concerned about guilt feelings, which I think are all too common in people generally, and maybe even especially within the church of Christ. It is my judgment that a great number of Christians do suffer under heavy guilt feelings. [10]

In the same article Eubanks quotes Paul Southern's observation:

> It is amazing how some Christians devote their energies in compulsive striving for moral and spiritual absolutism. The guilt feelings experienced by such persons are insoluble as long as they continue to strive for the impossible.[11]

O. H. Mowrer, a research psychologist, also is quoted as saying:

> There are, I conjecture, literally millions of Protestants who have followed Reformation theology as exactly as they knew how and still have found no deliverance from the onslaughts of an aggravated conscience. This ought not so to be.[12]

In the second of Eubanks' articles on "Unresolved Guilt in the Church," he names at least ten consequences of failure to show mercy to ourselves. They are listed here mostly as headings; the full contents can be obtained from Firm Foundation, Feb.15, 1977, article #2.

Eubanks asserts that unresolved guilt produces:

1) *A feeling of estrangement and alienation*—from God and others and breeds a permanent habit of withdrawal. The first thing Adam and Eve did when they felt their guilt was to hide.

---

[10] Ibid.

[11] Ibid.

[12] Ibid.

2) *Less fellowship in the church*. In a study of the self-actualization tendencies of seven religious groups on the campus of the University of Tennessee, Alfred Behel discovered that students who were members of the church of Christ tended to have low self-regard and a low capacity for intimate contact.

3) *The forfeiture of potentialities*. A person who constantly feels guilty will not be all he is capable of being.

4) *A habit of constant self-criticism*, which is often excessive, unrealistic and unnecessary.

5) *Efforts of self-imposed punishment*. In fact, self-criticism is a form of self-punishment.

6) *He will turn his guns on others*. The perpetually guilty [person] cannot stand all this criticism by himself, so…he will turn his guns on others.

7) *Will do away with all joy in the Christian life*. What is done as a Christian is done as a duty not as a joy.

8) *Greatly affects our hope of heaven*. And with a decrease in our hope, there is a decrease in activity, endurance and optimism. When asked, "Do you feel that personal unresolved guilt is one cause of a low level of evangelism on the part of members of the church?" 21 of the 39 preachers said "yes." Some bolstered it with "very definitely."

9) *The perpetually guilty are perpetually fearful*—not only of God, but of storms, accidents, loud noises, and such like.

10) *It affects many mentally and physically*.

   a. Guilt is thought to be at the very core of mental illness.
   b. The most drastic consequence is self-destruction: suicide.

So, "Blessed are the merciful" sits right at the heart of the Christian's life. Not to be merciful to oneself is tantamount to denying the grace of God. Though sometimes mistakenly viewed as humility, i.e., "I'm too evil for God to forgive me," it implies that God is not merciful, powerful or faithful enough to forgive all sin. Such is actually a misguided and strident display of pride and an expression of disbelief.

It is very possible that preachers, in large part, are responsible for this. In the rush to get people to the grave of baptism, some have minimized the fundamentals of faith and repentance and, in so doing, have buried "live" people instead of those who have died to sin through faith and repentance and thus are prepared for baptism.

During the 1960s some enthusiasts used an evangelistic method called "One Shot Evangelism." It advocated, simply put, that an evangelist knock on a door, greet the occupant, share the gospel and, right then and there, take the person and baptize him or her. In 1968 I was relating to a preacher friend how I had studied the gospel of John with a couple in New Zealand for a considerable number of weeks before they were baptized. Shocked at such delay, the friend asked me, "But what if they died before they got to the water?" I replied, "What if they died before they came to faith?"

I held back from him the rest of the story. After the study one evening, the man said, "I want to become a Christian; what must I do?" I replied, "I'm not going to tell you. I'll tell you where to find the answer and, if you really want to know, you can go there and find out for yourself." Then I bid them good night and left. I did this for two reasons: 1) I wasn't as concerned about their coming to the baptistery as I was concerned about their coming to faith. Wasn't that Jesus' instruction to Paul? "For Christ did not send me to baptize, but to preach the gospel…" (ICor.1:17) And 2) I didn't want their faith to be in my answer; I wanted them to find it for themselves. The next week he and his wife met me at their front door saying, "We've found it." They were baptized "the same hour of the night."

When, in our rush to get people to baptism, we bypass genuine faith and soul-rending repentance, we rob them of the experience which brings them to a clear conscience as they arise from baptism to walk the new life. Peter observed that "…baptism now saves you also—not the removal of dirt from the body but the *pledge of a good conscience toward God*" (I Pet. 3:21) (emphasis mine). Only a good conscience—trusting in God's faithfulness to forgive—allows one to be merciful to one's self and thus be equipped to show mercy to others.

These efforts to translate the Beatitudes into relationship language are attempts to connect the beatitude (which may be familiar to our ear but not always rooted in our heart) to actual verbal expressions. The translations attempt to give expression to emotions which are necessary in building, repairing and maintaining healthy relationships.

> ## *"Blessed are merciful" translated into Relationship Language:*

So, how does "Blessed are the merciful" translate into relationship language? If "Blessed are the poor in spirit" translates "I was wrong," and "Blessed are those who mourn" translates "I'm sorry," "Blessed are the merciful" naturally translates *"I forgive you."*

When someone has offended you but comes and humbly admits it and says "I'm sorry," the only Christ-like response will be, "I forgive you." Any response other than this will abort any effort to restore a healthy relationship. Only a hardened heart will rebuff a penitent admission of guilt and continue to stiff arm the offender and remain aloof and isolated. Three little words give solid substance to "I love you." They are, *"I forgive you."*

Chapter 7

"The Pure in Heart"

The Mask

Look at Me...I am a covering...
I hide expressions, feeling, tears
I do not cost money and for the
Most part, I am invisible to others.
I often appear early in life and I cling.
I AM A MASK!!

As a covering, I encourage people
To distort reality and perhaps live their
Entire lives for others...my way.
I am a dictator...I rule...
Oh, once in a while I give them a
Glimpse of what is real...but my
Substance is such that I am heavy
And difficult to shed.
I do not easily accept defeat, so
I remain in control
I AM A MASK!!

How long do I live…sometimes
The entire life of the person I am
Attached to…You see, I thrive on
The past…on mistakes…on fears or
Hurt…and I grow…However, occasionally
I contract a disease called acceptance and
Peace…and I grow weak…my smile leaves
And my outline becomes torn and tattered.
When this happens, I leave…I fade away
And search for someone else to attach
Myself to…someone who has not yet learned
Acceptance and peace…someone who
Is miserable, lost and drowning…just
Like me!
I will live forever…because I always
Have the power to return.
I AM A MASK!!

Carolyn Casto Fuller

THERE WAS A MAN out of work. He had exhausted his search for a job. But one day the circus came to town. The man went to the circus manager and asked if there was a job opening. The manager said, "Well, you're in luck. Our man who plays the part of the gorilla is sick. Do you want the job?" "What's involved?" asked the applicant. "You just wear this gorilla suit and swing out over the lion's cage on a rope and make the sound of a gorilla." "That's doable," the man thought, so he took the job.

On opening night he donned his gorilla suit, climbed the pole overlooking the lion's cage, grabbed the rope and swung out over the lion's cage. Thus began his gorilla routine. He really got into the swing of things…until he lost his grip on the rope and landed flat of his back in the lion's cage. The crowd gasped in horror as the lion came charging toward the gorilla. The gorilla came to and opened his mouth to scream for help. Suddenly a paw of the lion clamped down over the gorilla's mouth and, out of the mouth of the lion came a human voice, "Keep quiet or we'll both lose our jobs!"

Masks!! We all wear them at times—some maybe all the time. In this sixth beatitude, "Blessed are the pure in heart," Jesus invites us to take off our masks and be genuine, to put an end to duplicity and be single-minded. He calls us away from hypocrisy to transparency—to be the same on the inside as we appear to be on the outside. If it could be said of any of the beatitudes that 'this one expresses all the rest,' it would be this one that deals with the heart. The very call to 'repent' with which Jesus introduced his ministry implies the human heart is not pure. An ancient Jewish proverb affirms the importance of the heart: "Above all else, guard your heart, for it is the wellspring of life." (Prov.4:23)

"Extra! Extra! Read all about it: Jehovah to establish new covenant with Israel!" Thus would have read the headlines of the *Jerusalem Journal* seven hundred years earlier. The difference between the old covenant and the projected new covenant was that the new covenant would be "put in their minds and written on their hearts." (Jer.31:31-34) No longer would an infant be ceremonially inducted into a covenant without his knowledge or consent, and later be taught what that ceremony implied. In the new covenant, "they will all know me, from the least to the greatest," declares the Lord, "for I will forgive their wickedness and will remember their sins no more."

The new covenant rules out the induction of an infant because the infant's heart is not involved, and he has committed no sins for which to be forgiven. It also prohibits naively assuming that, just because an adult has been immersed, he/she is a Christian regardless the condition of the heart.

We would be surprised if Jesus had not made the heart the heart of his message. Our hearts need renovating and purifying. Actually we need a heart transplant, not stints or by-pass surgery; we need a whole new heart. Jesus declared to his contemporaries: "You hypocrites! Isaiah was right when he prophesied about you:"

> These people honor me with their lips,
>> but their hearts are far from me.
> They worship me in vain;
>> their teachings are but rules taught by men.
>
> Isa.29:13

They were 'correct on the outside but corrupt on the inside.' (Mt.23:25-28)

> Make a tree good and its fruit will be good, or make a tree bad and its fruit will be bad. You brood of vipers, how can you who are evil say anything good? For from the overflow of the heart the mouth speaks. (12:33, 34)

The universal diagnosis is very discouraging: "The heart is deceitful above all things, and desperately corrupt," said Jeremiah. (17:9) Jesus makes the same diagnosis: "Out of the heart come evil thoughts, murder, adultery, sexual immorality, theft, false testimony, slander." (Mt.15:19) "Enough, already!!" you may be thinking. "What's the use?!"

Just here we need a word or two of encouragement: First, purity of heart does not come to us overnight; long-held thought patterns do not die easily. The apostle Paul, in his letter to the Philippian church, expressed a desire, made some surprising admissions and then gave some very practical advice on maturing in Christ.

First, he expressed a desire to know Christ:

> I want to know Christ—yes, to know the power of his resurrection and participation in his sufferings, becoming like him in his death, and so, somehow, attaining to the resurrection from the dead. (Phil.3:10, 11)

But then he admitted:

> Not that I have already obtained all this, or have already arrived at my goal, but I press on to take hold of that for which Christ Jesus took hold of me. Brothers and sisters, I do not consider myself yet to have taken hold of it. But one thing I do: Forgetting what is behind and straining toward what is ahead, I press on toward the goal to win the prize for which God has called me heavenward in Christ Jesus. (3:12-14)

Then, as a general rule for all, he advised:

> All of us, then, who are mature should take such a view of things. And if on some point you think differently, that too God will make clear to you. Only let us live up to what we have already attained. (vv.15, 16)

Paul concluded with this advice: *'Guard your thoughts.'*

> Finally, brothers and sisters, whatever is true, whatever is noble, whatever is right, whatever is pure, whatever is lovely, whatever is admirable—if anything is excellent or praiseworthy—think about such things. (4:8,9)

There are two suggested disciplines that may help implement Paul's advice to "think about such things."

1) **Practice the "21 Day Rule."** Think pure thoughts twenty one days in a row, and you'll likely find it easier to keep on thinking pure thoughts. Repeated thoughts create "crevices" in the brain. The longer the thoughts are entertained, the deeper the crevice. So:

> Watch your thoughts, for they become words.
> Watch your words, for they become actions.
> Watch your actions, for they become habits.
> Watch your habits, for they become character.
> Watch your character, for it becomes your destiny.

> (author unknown)

2) **Then, be conscious of the progression of godliness** as it develops from ungodliness to godliness. (This model is adapted from a learning procedure pioneered by the US Gordan Training International organization.)[13] It includes four levels of awareness:

   a) *Unconscious Incompetence*—'you don't know that you don't know.'
   b) *Conscious Incompetence*—'you know that you don't know.'
   c) *Conscious Competence*—'you know that you know.'
   d) *Unconscious Competence*—'you don't know that you know;' it just comes easily and unconsciously, like breathing. It is 'involuntary.'

Using this model, I have constructed a parallel path to godliness.

First, there is *Unconscious ungodliness*—A condition in which one is not aware of his ungodliness.

Second, there is *Conscious ungodliness*—The conscience, having been educated, is aware of its ungodliness.

Third, there is *Conscious godliness*—This is "cognitive determination" to do what is right or godly. Admirable, but not the desired destination.

---

[13] W. C. Howell & E. A. Fleishman (eds). *Human Productivity. Vol.2*, (Hillsdale, NJ: Earlbaum, 1982).

Fourth, there is *Unconscious godliness*—This condition reflects godliness at a level which is "involuntary," i.e., godliness becomes as natural as breathing. This godliness is no longer a cognitive decision but a morally ingrained reflex or "purity of heart."

Here's an interesting caveat: Coming closer to God should make us feel more godly, shouldn't it? Strangely enough, the closer one comes to God the more aware one becomes of just how ungodly one is. It's like a coal miner—as he gets closer to the light he becomes increasingly aware of just how covered he is with dirt and coal dust.

But this is no problem for the believer. Just as coming increasingly closer to God (the Light) makes us aware of how unclean we are, so drawing closer to God in faith makes us increasingly aware of how cleansed we are. For, "If we walk in the light as he is in the light, we have fellowship with one another, and the blood of Jesus, his Son, purifies us from all sin." (I John 1:7)

So, take heart: Purity of heart is within reach of all who come to God through Christ.

"Blessed are the Pure in Heart" translated into Relationship Language:

In relation to God, purity of heart is singleness of devotion. God himself has translated it: ***"You shall have no other gods besides me."*** (Ex.20:3) Jesus insisted, ***"You cannot serve both God and money."*** (Lk.16:13)

In relation to other humans—especially in the marriage relationship—I would translate it something like this: ***"I love you only, and I trust you completely."*** Purity of heart delivers one from deceit—there is no illicit lover waiting in a bed in some other location. Purity of heart frees one also from suspicion that the other partner may be doing that very thing or something worse.

In relation to self, let Polonius define it: *"This above all: to thine own self be true."* [14] Indeed, "Above all else, guard your heart, for it is the wellspring of life." (Prov.4:23)

---

[14] (Hamlet Act 1, scene 3, 78–82).

Chapter 8

"The Peacemakers"

Peace in the World

If there is to be peace in the world,
There must be peace in the nations.
If there is to be peace in the nations,
There must be peace in the cities.
If there is to be peace in the cities,
There must be peace between neighbors.
If there is to be peace between neighbors,
There must be peace in the home.
If there is to be peace in the home,
There must be peace in the heart.

Lao Tzu

As true as Lao Tzu's observations are, they are inadequate since they do not reveal the *way* to peace. The "If" and "There must be" are empty platitudes since the *way* to peace is not revealed. A final line in Lao Tzu's poem would make it complete: "If there is to be peace in the heart, that heart must be anchored in Jesus Christ." There will be world peace only when the world comes to know and submit to the Prince of Peace—Jesus Christ. Seven hundred years before angels announced "Peace on earth, good will to men," the Hebrew prophet Isaiah foresaw the special event:

> For to us a child is born, to us a son is given, and the government will be on his shoulders. And he will be called Wonderful Counselor, Mighty God, Everlasting Father, Prince of Peace. (Isa.9:6)

This "Prince of Peace" brought, and continues to bring, peace on three levels. First and foremost is **Peace with God**. There can be no peace on any other level without peace with God. There may be uneasy truces in which there is temporary cessation of hostility, but no true peace exists without being at peace with God. The human race was at peace with God until sin entered the world. At that moment a separation occurred—Adam and Eve knew that something had occurred that made them hide from God (Gen. 3:6-8). God knew it, and he came looking for them (3:9). Adam and Eve, of course, began the blame game (3:10-12), Eve blaming the serpent and Adam blaming Eve and God—"the woman you gave me…" And so began the insidious spread of sin until, in Peterson's graphic description:

> You know the story of how Adam landed us in the dilemma we're in—first sin, then death, and no one exempt from either sin or death. That sin disturbed relations with God in every thing and everyone, but the extent of the disturbance was not clear until God spelled it out in detail to Moses. So death, this huge abyss separating us from God, dominated the landscape from Adam to Moses. Even those who didn't sin precisely as Adam did by disobeying a specific command of God still had to experience this termination of life, this separation from God. (Rom. 5:12-14, *The Message*)

That "abyss" opened with Adam and Eve and continued to deepen in the deteriorating human scene until the chasm was so deep and wide God was sorry he had made man. He decided to wipe off the face of the earth every human that breathed—in fact—everything that had the breath of life was destined for destruction:

> The LORD saw how great man's wickedness on the earth had become, and that every inclination of the thoughts of his heart was only evil all the time. The LORD was grieved that he had made man on the earth, and his heart was filled with pain. So the LORD said, "I will wipe mankind, whom I have created, from the face of the earth—men and animals, and creatures that move along the ground, and birds of the air—for I am grieved that I have made them." (Gen.5:6-7)

Fortunately, a man by the name of Noah found favor in the eyes of the Lord (Gen.5:8). With this man, his wife, three sons and their wives Jehovah made a new start and gave the human race a second chance, promising never again to destroy the whole earth with water (9:11). Jehovah promised this "even though every inclination of [man's] heart is evil from childhood." (8:21) The ensuing record of this planet's inhabitants confirms that sad assessment as generation after generation repeated the sins of their fathers. This spiritual genetic defect continually occurred and increased even among God's chosen people until "there was no remedy." (2Chron. 36:16b)

Isaiah pointed to the condition and its cause:

> Surely the arm of the LORD is not too short to save,
>   nor his ear too dull to hear.
> But your iniquities have separated
>   you from your God;
> your sins have hidden his face from you,
>   so that he will not hear. (Isa.59:1,2)

Jesus, the Prince of Peace, came and bridged the chasm with his cross and restored man to God, thus making peace "through his blood, shed on the cross." (Col. 1:20)

Peace with God having thus been restored through Christ, a second level of peace became operative: **Peace with self**. This is not just human conjecture. Every letter Paul wrote began with this salutation, "Grace and peace" and in that order—grace first, then peace. Peter followed the same order in both his letters. It is only after grace has been experienced that peace with self can be enjoyed. Paul's prayers for the churches included "Now may the Lord of peace himself give you peace at all times and in every way. The Lord be with all of you." (2 Thess. 3:16) To the Romans he concluded with this prayer: "May the God of hope fill you with all joy and peace as you trust in him, so that you may overflow with hope by the power of the Holy Spirit." (Rom. 15:13)

I just finished the book **Unbroken** by Laura Hillenbrand. It is the true story of Lieutenant Louis Zamperini who, after competing in the Berlin Olympics, was caught up in World War II. After surviving the crash of his aircraft he spent 43 days on the Pacific Ocean in a small, two-man life raft—with two other men—clinging to life. Captured by the Japanese, he suffered a year and a half in unbelievably inhuman conditions in Japanese prison camps under the most brutal treatment—especially at the hands of a guard the prisoners named the "Bird."

Finally set free after VJ day in August 1945, Lt. Zamperini began a life of emotional bondage brought on by the scars of the war. It drove him to alcoholism and to the near-destruction of his marriage and his life. He couldn't get free of the Bird. He became violent; flashbacks tormented him. While living in such a hell, he reluctantly agreed to go with his wife to a Billy Graham crusade in Los Angeles. Sitting there listening to the gospel, he suddenly felt frantic beyond control. He rushed out of the meeting, fleeing from the "demons" that were tormenting him. He was filled with hate for those who had tortured him. Though free from the Japanese prisons, he still was in prison—a captive of his own hate.

His wife begged him to go back to the Graham meeting once more. Against his will he conceded and went with her. The sermon for the evening was on John chapter 8 (the woman taken in adultery). Panicking again he started to run but, overcome by the love of God he saw in Jesus, he turned around instead and responded to the invitation. He went home that night, poured out all his alcohol, threw away his cigarettes, and for the first night in three years slept through the night in total peace. He was finally free of the "Bird."

Louis Zamperini lived into his nineties, giving the rest of his life to serving young men in a camp he had built for disadvantaged youth. All of this he did because he had found peace in Christ.

There is a third level of peace to which the Prince of Peace brings us. It is the **Peace we enjoy with others**—even our enemies. Lt. Zamperini found he no longer felt hatred for his enemies; instead he felt compassion. He went back to Japan and asked to meet those who had served as guards at the prisons. He sat before an audience of hundreds of imprisoned war criminals. At first he didn't recognize any of them. But then, at the back of the large room, he saw four of those who had mistreated him. He pointed them out, and the four were ordered to come forward. They stood and hesitatingly started walking toward him, unsure what to expect from him. Welling up within him was not hate but a profound sense of compassion. He ran to them with outstretched arms and embraced them in forgiveness. Lt. Zamperini had finally won the larger war!

Peace is the most obvious sociological blessing Christ offers the world. It is the "peace on earth, good will to man." It is the life-giving peace between people—spouses, neighbors, strangers, and even enemies. This peace is not accidental; it was the intentional result God had planned long ago before it became a reality in Christ.

> For he himself is our peace, who has made the two one and has destroyed the barrier, the dividing wall of hostility, by abolishing in his flesh the law with its commandments and regulations. His purpose was to create in himself one new man out of the two, thus making peace, and in this one body to reconcile both of them to God through the cross, by which he put to death their hostility. He came and preached peace to you who were far away and peace to those who were near. For through him we both have access to the Father by one Spirit. (Ephesians 2:14-18)

The most pressing need on earth today is peace. Hatred, animosity, ill will, and alienation are destroying the human race in every corner of the globe. If we would only submit our wills to the Prince of Peace, all the animosity would cease and peace would reign. His purpose was to create such a colony of peace on earth where we...

> ...are no longer foreigners and aliens, but fellow citizens with God's people and members of God's household, built on the foundation of the apostles and prophets, with Christ Jesus

himself as the chief cornerstone. In him the whole building is joined together and rises to become a holy temple in the Lord. And in him you too are being built together to become a dwelling in which God lives by his Spirit. (2:19-22)

Jesus doesn't call his followers to be peace *lovers* but to be peace *makers*. This calls for effort and action on our part. Nor does he call us to just a nebulous, undefined road to peace as though it were easily acquired or naturally maintained. In the remainder of the Sermon on the Mount he gives definite instructions which provide clarity for application. He calls us:

From anger and violence to RECONCILIATION:

> You have heard that it was said to the people long ago, 'Do not murder, and anyone who murders will be subject to judgment.' But I tell you that anyone who is angry with his brother will be subject to judgment. Again, anyone who says to his brother, 'Raca,' is answerable to the Sanhedrin. But anyone who says, 'You fool!' will be in danger of the fire of hell. Therefore, if you are offering your gift at the altar and there remember that your brother has something against you, leave your gift there in front of the altar. First go and be reconciled to your brother; then come and offer your gift. (Matt. 5:21-24)

From adultery and divorce to FAITHFUL RELATIONSHIPS:

> You have heard that it was said, 'Do not commit adultery.' But I tell you that anyone who looks at a woman lustfully has already committed adultery with her in his heart. (5:27) It has been said, 'Anyone who divorces his wife must give her a certificate of divorce.' But I tell you that anyone who divorces his wife, except for marital unfaithfulness, causes her to become an adulteress, and anyone who marries the divorced woman commits adultery. (5:31, 32)

From dishonesty and falsehood to TRUTH:

> ...you have heard that it was said to the people long ago, 'Do not break your oath, but keep the oaths you have made to the

Lord.' But I tell you, Do not swear at all: either by heaven, for it is God's throne; or by the earth, for it is his footstool; or by Jerusalem, for it is the city of the Great King. And do not swear by your head, for you cannot make even one hair white or black. Simply let your 'Yes' be 'Yes,' and your 'No,' 'No'; anything beyond this comes from the evil one. (5:33-37)

From revenge to GOING THE SECOND MILE:

You have heard that it was said, 'Eye for eye, and tooth for tooth.' But I tell you, Do not resist an evil person. If someone strikes you on the right cheek, turn to him the other also. And if someone wants to sue you and take your tunic, let him have your cloak as well. If someone forces you to go one mile, go with him two miles. Give to the one who asks you, and do not turn away from the one who wants to borrow from you. (5:38-42)

From hate to LOVE OF ENEMIES:

You have heard that it was said, 'Love your neighbor and hate your enemy.' But I tell you: Love your enemies and pray for those who persecute you, that you may be sons of your Father in heaven. He causes his sun to rise on the evil and the good, and sends rain on the righteous and the unrighteous. If you love those who love you, what reward will you get? Are not even the tax collectors doing that? And if you greet only your brothers, what are you doing more than others? Do not even pagans do that? (5:43-37)

From religious pride to HUMILITY:

Be careful not to do your 'acts of righteousness' before men, to be seen by them. If you do, you will have no reward from your Father in heaven. So when you give to the needy, do not announce it with trumpets, as the hypocrites do in the synagogues and on the streets, to be honored by men. I tell you the truth, they have received their reward in full. But when you give to the needy, do not let your left hand know what your right hand is doing, so that your giving may be in secret. Then your Father, who sees what is done in secret, will reward you. And when you pray, do not be like the hypocrites, for they love to pray standing in the synagogues and on the street corners to be seen by men. I tell you the truth, they have received their reward in full. But when you pray, go into your room, close the door and pray to your Father, who is unseen. Then your Father, who sees what is done in secret, will reward you. And when you pray, do not keep on babbling like pagans, for they think they will be heard because of their many words. Do not be like them, for your Father knows what you need before you ask him. (6:5-8)

From materialism and anxiety to TRUST IN GOD:

Do not store up for yourselves treasures on earth, where moth and rust destroy, and where thieves break in and steal. But store up for yourselves treasures in heaven, where moth and rust do not destroy, and where thieves do not break in and steal. For where your treasure is, there your heart will be also. The eye is the lamp of the body. If your eyes are good, your whole body will be full of light. But if your eyes are bad, your whole body will be full of darkness. If then the light within you is darkness, how great is that darkness! No one can serve two masters. Either he will hate the one and love the other, or he will be devoted to the one and despise the other. You cannot serve both God and Money. (6:19-24)

From judgment to MERCY:

Do not judge, or you too will be judged. For in the same way you judge others, you will be judged, and with the measure you use, it will be measured to you. "Why do you look at the speck of sawdust in your brother's eye and pay no attention to the plank in your own eye? How can you say to your brother, 'Let me take the speck out of your eye,' when all the time there is a plank in your own eye? You hypocrite, first take the plank out of your own eye, and then you will see clearly to remove the speck from your brother's eye. (7:1-5)

"Blessed are the peacemakers" is the apex of the Beatitudes. All the others lead up to it. "Well," someone may say, "If it is so important, why is it not listed first?" The answer is fairly simple: One isn't prepared to be a peacemaker until the other qualities mentioned prior to peacemaking are present in one's life: Reconciliation, Faithful Relationships, Truthfulness, Going the Second Mile, Love of Enemies, Humility, and Trust in God. These qualities equip a person to be a peace maker.

Surprisingly, however, the seeds of peacemaking sometimes lie nascent and blossom prematurely, appearing in their own time and seemingly out of place. But early or late, Jesus leads his followers into the new life of peace, patterned after and made possible by the Prince of Peace.

There are five identifiable steps in being a peacemaker. The first principle of peacemaking is: ***"Take the First Step."***

> Therefore, if you are offering your gift at the altar and there remember that your brother has something against you, leave your gift there in front of the altar. First go and be reconciled to your brother; then come and offer your gift. (Mt. 5:23, 24)

Some years ago I was involved in an interim preaching assignment with a church in Texas. While there, a member by the name of Larry Doaks received a call from a former business associate Mike Anderson. Mike said, "Larry, I've just been diagnosed with liver cancer. I have no faith, but I have noticed in our dealings over the years that you do. Would you come out and tell me about your faith?" Larry said, "Of course I'll come." He took the next plane to his friend Mike's house in Phoenix, AZ. It was a Friday afternoon. Arriving at Mike's home, he spent the rest of the day and into the night telling Mike the good news.

The next day (Saturday) they bought the movie on the Gospel of John and watched the whole story of the life of Jesus. At the conclusion Mike said, "That makes sense." The next day Mike accompanied Larry to church, and as the Lord's Supper was being served, Mike asked Larry, "Is this for everyone?" Larry answered, "It's for believers." With some hesitation Mike took the bread, looked at it thoughtfully—first at the bread, then looking upward and back to the bread in his hand. He then, with resolution, placed it in his mouth. When the cup was served, he took it without hesitation and drank. He had made up his mind: he believed.

After the service ended, Mike said to Larry, "I want to be baptized…but not right now. I need some time; I've got some things to take care of first."

During that week Mike sat down and made a list of all the people he could remember having offended and also those who had offended him. He called each one of them and apologized for whatever were the offenses and either forgave or asked them for forgiveness. Word got around that something strange was going on. Calls began to come to Larry reporting the strange behavior of Mike Anderson. A friend called Mike and asked, "What's going on? Why are you making all these calls?" Mike shared his new found faith in Christ with each contact and gave this explanation for his conciliatory calling: "I don't believe God will forgive me if I'm not willing to forgive others." Having accomplished that, he was baptized. And so continued Mike's faith walk with God.

But that's not the end of the story. Mike lived two more years and became heavily involved with the church, serving others and sharing his faith. At his funeral some amazing things took place. The church anticipated some 500 friends would attend, and they did—musicians with whom Mike had performed drove up in limousines, representatives of Martial Arts also were present, friends he knew, many he didn't know but who knew him. In all, around a thousand people showed up. Larry Doak went to the funeral thinking there would be perhaps an hour's service. Larry later reported to me that the funeral lasted five hours! So many wanted to testify about the influence Mike Anderson had had on them. What could be done but let them speak? And speak they did!

And Mike also, though dead, still speaks. Every year since Mike's death his martial arts friends have observed a memorial in honor of this two-year-old follower of the Prince of Peace. He was no longer a 'foreigner or an alien but a fellow citizen with God's people and a member of God's household, built on the foundation of the apostles and prophets, with Christ Jesus himself as the chief cornerstone' of his life. He had become a 'dwelling place in which God lived by his Spirit.' (Eph.2:19-22)

The second principle of peacemaking is: ***"Go the second mile."***

> You have heard that it was said, 'Eye for eye, and tooth for tooth.' But I tell you, Do not resist an evil person. If someone strikes you on the right cheek, turn to him the other

also. And if someone wants to sue you and take your tunic,
let him have your cloak as well. If someone forces you to go
one mile, go with him two miles. (5:38-41)

One day there was a knock on my office door. There stood a rough-looking
man with one hand missing. Paul Healey was unkempt and uneasy. He was
asking for help to "get on down the road." Preachers often get the honor of
handling benevolent cases—not always regarded an honor. But I listened
to Paul's case. He had just been released from prison and needed a tire and
a tank of gas. I went with him as a representative of the church. While he
was filling up his tank I watched the attendant put a good used tire on the
right rear of Paul's car. I noticed the left rear tire—it looked as bad as the
one just replaced. I told the station attendant, "Put another tire on the left
rear; the one he has isn't going to make it very far down the road." So the
attendant did. Then I said to Paul, "One tank of gas isn't going to get you
where you're going." So I gave him enough money (not mine, the church's)
to fill his tank again. He thanked me and off he drove.

About an hour later there was another knock on my door. I opened it and
there stood Paul Healey again. I invited him in. This is what he said: "Well, as
I drove down the road I realized that I wanted to live among people who treat
others like I've been treated. This is where I'm going stay." So he did. Some
time later he came to believe in Jesus, and I baptized him. He had no social
skills; he had little or no Bible knowledge. He had mostly an honest heart, a
hot temper and an itch to get on down the road. He never got over the itch,
but he stayed long enough to get a glimpse of Jesus and people who would go
the second mile for others, and he wanted to be a part of that.

A few years later the itch got to him, and he moved on. But we kept in
touch by mail. I sent him materials to help him grow in his faith. His letters, misspelled words by the handful, continued to come and were filled
with genuine words reflecting his faith as it grew more and more with the
passing of years. I don't know if he is still alive or not, but he came alive in
Christ by witnessing followers of Jesus going the second mile.

Paul Healey, uneducated ex-convict turned Christian, taught me something:
I'm convinced the most good that comes from our benevolence is what we
do *beyond* what those in need ask of us. "But, you'll get ripped off if you give
like that!" I know. And when I reported to the elders what I had done, the

treasurer exclaimed, "If we act like that, there won't *be* any Benevolence Fund left!!" But our Father causes his sun to rise on the evil and the good. He is kind to even the ungrateful (Lk.6:35), and we're told to be like him. When we settle to act otherwise, his question, "What are you doing more than others?" should haunt us. I don't know all the answers, but I've seen the results of going the second mile, and I'm convinced it works—along with "turning the other cheek," etc. The risk is there. Loving the unlovely is always a risk, but God does it every time he gives to us, and he calls on us to follow his example. If we don't, "What *are* we doing more than others?"

The third principle of peacemaking is: "***Don't wear your feelings on your sleeve.***" Are you aware that there is no record of Jesus ever taking offense at anything done to him? He took offense only if his Father was deprived of his honor or people were robbed of their needs. Then, you'd better watch out; 'all heaven would break loose!' Remember when he cleaned the temple? "How dare you turn my Father's house into a market!" Or when the woman afflicted with scoliosis for eighteen years would have been put off until sundown or some other of the six days on which men were allowed to work? "You hypocrites! Which of you having an ox or a donkey will not lead him away on the Sabbath to water? Should not this woman whom Satan has bound for low these eighteen years be loosed from her bonds on the Sabbath?" (Lk.13:15, 16) Let God be deprived of his honor or people of their needs and you'd better get out of the way.

Yes, Jesus never took offense at anything done to himself. How different that is from the way we humans usually act. We tend to take offense *only* when something is done to us. We so often wear our feelings on our sleeves, ready to take offense at the slightest hurt. In the film *A Stroke of Genius* (a story about Bobby Jones—perhaps the greatest golfer who ever lived) there is a scene in his law office that is amusing and amazing. Bobby Jones, being an amateur, never took money for playing golf. He made his living as a lawyer. One day a man burst into Bobby Jones' law office, red faced and angry. "I'm going to sue his britches off," shouted the man. Jones asked the man to sit down and tell him the reason he was angry enough to sue. The angry man blurted out, "He told me to go to hell!" Jones listened, then calmly said, "Well, I would advise you just to let it pass." "No!" said the man. "He told me to go to hell!" Jones then said, "Well, I've checked the law on that, and …you don't have to go!" When that statement registered with the angry man, you could just see his anger fade away: his shoulders relaxed, and he let it pass as Bobby Jones advised. He "took his feelings off his sleeve."

The fourth principle of peacemaking is: *"Serve rather than be served."* Here's the scene: twenty-six dirty feet—dirty from walking through dirt, dung and dust on the streets of Jerusalem. The droppings of animals brought by pilgrims for sacrifice filled the streets where everyone walked in open sandals. The twenty-six dirty feet belonged to Jesus and his twelve disciples—all ringed around the table waiting for the evening meal. The disciples were arguing about who among them was the greatest (Lk.22:24). This was their concern on this last night of their Lord's earthly life. Surely, after being with the Prince of Peace for over three years, this was not still being debated!! But it was. Peace was still tenuous and unity of the group still had not formed.

This was the last night. He had modeled peace before them for three years. It was very late to be trying once more to show them the path to peace. What would he do? He was their Lord; how could he show them?

> It was just before the Passover Feast. Jesus knew that the time had come for him to leave this world and go to the Father. Having loved his own who were in the world, he now showed them the full extent of his love.
>
> The evening meal was being served, and the devil had already prompted Judas Iscariot, son of Simon, to betray Jesus. Jesus knew that the Father had put all things under his power, and that he had come from God and was returning to God; so he got up from the meal, took off his outer clothing, and wrapped a towel around his waist. After that, he poured water into a basin and began to wash his disciples' feet, drying them with the towel that was wrapped around him. (John 13:1-5)

Jesus' action stunned his disciples and shamed them. They should have been the ones serving him! Yet, here he was—their Lord, doing the job of a lowly servant. The twelve were caught in their prideful resistance to perform such a humble service. Jesus had once again turned life's picture right-side up. "He who humbles himself shall be exalted." (Lk. 18:14) And, "If anyone would be first, he must be servant of all." (Mk. 9:35)

After returning to his place at the table, he asked the Twelve: "Do you understand what I have done for you?"

> You call me 'Teacher' and 'Lord,' and rightly so, for that is what
> I am. Now that I, your Lord and Teacher, have washed your
> feet, you also should wash one another's feet. (Jn.13:13, 14)

Three truths empowered Jesus to stoop and wash the feet of his disciples. Verse 3 reveals these: "Jesus knew that the Father had put all things under his power, and that he had come from God and was returning to God." He was aware of 1) who he was, 2) from whence he had come and 3) where he was going. Having this knowledge of himself he was able to serve those who should have been serving him. Being aware of these same three truths (knowing who we are, where we came from and where we are going) will enable us also to serve those around us.

Love is the fifth principle of peacemaking and is that quality which makes all the other qualities possible. John chapter 13 raises the curtain on this scene and records this dramatic show of humble service:

> Jesus knew that the time had come for him to leave this world
> and go to the Father. Having loved his own who were in the
> world, he now showed them the full extent of his love. (v.1)

Only divine love equipped Jesus to serve as he did. And love is the only thing that will equip you and me to do the same. The importance of love is seen in the fact that in his humble action he gave them both an example and a command to do the same as he had done.

> I have set you an example that you should do as I have done
> for you. I tell you the truth, no servant is greater than his
> master, nor is a messenger greater than the one who sent
> him. Now that you know these things, you will be blessed if
> you do them. (vv. 15-17)

Dare we ignore both the example and the command of our Lord? Humble service to others is his example and command. Washing feet was that culture's way of demonstrating humble service to others. There are dedicated followers of Christ today who believe washing feet is a custom to be followed by all believers for all time. Whatever may be your understanding of Jesus' action, let your life be a living example of serving others rather than being served. This is the way to peace.

Making peace implies two parties and requires two complimentary mindsets. In all resolutions of conflict there must be 1) an initiator and 2) a reciprocator. Somebody has to "break the ice." Someone must get the ball rolling toward the goal. That person is known as the initiator. Without an initiator nothing good will happen, and without a willing reciprocator nothing good will continue; there will be a log jam. It's interesting that an initiator and a reciprocator often end up marrying each other! "Opposites attract." If "politics makes strange bedfellows," so does marriage.

> ## *"Blessed are the Peacemakers" translated into Relationship Language:*

But, how does "Blessed are the peacemakers" translate into human relationship language? There are many ways that initiators indicate their willingness to bury the hatchet (somewhere other than in the other's head!). A wife may bake her husband his favorite cake; a husband may bring his wife a box of candy or a bouquet of flowers. Or just a touch of the hand may be all that is needed to indicate the war is over. However you say it or do it, it must come across something like this: ***"Let me be the first to make up."*** Those who have been married for any length of time—short or long –know the welcome relief which comes when an offer is made (by an initiator) and is accepted (by a willing reciprocator). Peace once more reigns in the home.

Years ago, after preaching on this subject, my wife and I were driving home after the morning church service. Louine asked me, "Jimmy John," (what she calls me at times) "am I a willing reciprocator?" I answered her, "Tewanis" (a special name with a story), "you are to me like a gentle ocean breeze…with sudden gusts of a hundred miles an hour!" That little blue, thirteen year-old Volkswagen just sort of floated on to the house.

There's nothing better than peace. The promised result of such a dance best describes its importance: "…for they will be called sons of God."

Chapter 9

"The Persecuted For Righteousness"

THE first and eighth beatitudes form "bookends" for the other six sayings. These two: "Blessed are the poor in spirit," and "Blessed are those who are persecuted for righteousness" have as the stated result, "For theirs is the kingdom of heaven." Bold though it may seem, I suggest these eight sayings represent the mindset of the kingdom of God, the reign of Christ, the mind of God. As noted in Chapter 1, they serve as a virtual autobiography of the man who spoke them. They are the component parts of the unapproachable light in which God the Creator lives. They are the 'essence of the essence' of the teachings of Christ. All else that Jesus taught flows from them as does everything which the Spirit later revealed in the writings of the Apostles. So important were these sayings and their implications that he asserted:

> Therefore everyone who hears these words of mine and puts them into practice is like a wise man who built his house on the rock. The rain came down, the streams rose, and the winds blew and beat against that house; yet it did not fall, because it had its foundation on the rock. But everyone who hears these words of mine and does not put them into practice is like a foolish man who built his house on sand. The rain came down, the streams rose, and the winds blew and beat against that house, and it fell with a great crash. (Mt.7:24-27)

Jesus' life consisted of these principles. He embodied them. They were the warp and woof of his earthly existence. He asks nothing more of us than what he exemplified in his own life. And so, we come to the last of these

71

eight sayings, "Blessed are those who are persecuted for righteousness, for theirs is the kingdom of heaven." As with the others, we scratch our heads and ask, "What's he talking about?" Surely, there can't be blessing in persecution. But there is.

Instead of attempting to editorialize or speculate on its meaning, I have decided simply to hold up Jesus and gaze at his handling of persecution. In doing so, we realize that what he is showing us is '*how to suffer unjust treatment without losing our joy.*' We see this attribute in his life recorded in the Gospels. We see the kingly serenity with which he bore his sufferings and mistreatment. Later on, 1st century writers record what they themselves had seen first hand of Christ's suffering or had heard of it from others. The author of Hebrews, for one, refers to Christ's triumphant suffering, saying "Let us fix our eyes on Jesus, the author and perfecter of our faith, who for the joy set before him endured the cross, scorning its shame, and sat down at the right hand of the throne of God." (12:2)

But specifically for this chapter we are going to view the concept of suffering unjustly through the eyes of an eye witness of Jesus' suffering: Simon Peter. Thirty years after Jesus had ascended, Peter still remembered how Jesus had bourn up under severe persecution and had left us an example that we should follow in his steps (IPet.2:21). He cites Isa.53:9 that "He committed no sin, and no deceit was found in his mouth." Peter goes into some detail, telling us that "When they hurled insults at him, he did not retaliate; when he suffered he made no threats." These statements tell us *what* he did but give very little indication as to *how* he did it, only to say, "Instead, he entrusted himself to him who judges justly." (v.23b) Peter again mentions the fact of Jesus' suffering in 4:1. "Since Christ suffered in his body, arm yourselves with the same attitude." And there's the key: Jesus had an "attitude" toward suffering that brought him through triumphantly. His attitude allowed him to suffer unjustly without losing his joy.

But, for years I missed the lesson on suffering. I missed it because I had considered suffering only as physical persecution. I had in mind beatings, scourgings, prison, etc. During those years there was no such suffering being endured by Christians—at least not in America. It may come to that, but I had no concept of such at the time. I finally realized there are other kinds of suffering such as emotional, financial, social, relational etc. Having come to this broader perception, I was able to come to grips with a suffering which more accurately reflects the reality of life in any circumstance.

But what was that attitude which brought Jesus through persecution and will do the same for us today? Before we answer that question, notice how broad the application is to the life of a believer. In Peter's first letter, he addressed the subject of suffering a total of 20 times. He reminded his readers that what they were suffering was not some strange phenomenon happening only to them but was happening also to their brothers and sisters throughout the world (IPet.5:9). Furthermore, he observed that the unjust suffering was caused by 'unequal relationships.' Specifically, he pointed out the three areas where unjust treatment would most likely occur: 1) as subjects of the government of Rome, 2) at work and 3) at home. It was in these "unequal" relationships that Peter called the believers to imitate Jesus. In all honesty, every human relationship is *unequal*. It is precisely here that we are called to follow Jesus' example.

But, what did Jesus know about "unequal" relationships? The fact is—all Jesus knew in his life on earth were unequal relationships! Even with his own Twelve his relationship was almost always like oil and water; they never understood him or what he taught—unless he took them aside and explained his teachings. Even then, the warnings of his impending death and resurrection remained a puzzle to them. And when they finally came face to face with his suffering, they either crashed emotionally and went to sleep while he sweated blood in the garden or, terrified for their lives, they all left him and fled.

The nearest thing Jesus experienced among people that could be described as "equal" was in the home of Mary, Martha and Lazarus of Bethany. That home, it seems, was the one place where Jesus could 'take off his sandals' and feel at home. It was his 'home away from home.' But even there, on one occasion, the serenity of the moment was interrupted by a frustrated Martha coming through the kitchen door saying, "Lord, do you not care that Mary has left me to do all the serving?" Then she gave the Creator of the universe a curt command: "Tell her to come help me!" Even that didn't ruffle Jesus; he just said, 'Now, Martha, calm down. Mary has chosen the better part, and it won't be taken away from her.' (Lk.10:37-42) The only equal relationship Jesus had was with his Father.

The first area of unequal relationships Peter addressed to his contemporaries was with the Roman government. Regarding a Christian's relationship to the government, he said:

> Submit yourselves for the Lord's sake to every authority instituted among men: whether to the king, as the supreme authority, or to governors, who are sent by him to punish those who do wrong and to commend those who do right. For it is God's will that by doing good you should silence the ignorant talk of foolish men. Live as free men, but do not use your freedom as a cover-up for evil; live as servants of God. Show proper respect to everyone: Love the brotherhood of believers, fear God, honor the king. (IPet.2:13-17)

Jesus warned his own people of the consequences of their continuing resistance to Rome. He cited two examples for their consideration:

> Now there were some present at that time who told Jesus about the Galileans whose blood Pilate had mixed with their sacrifices. Jesus answered, "Do you think that these Galileans were worse sinners than all the other Galileans because they suffered this way? I tell you, no! But unless you repent, you too will all perish. Or those eighteen who died when the tower in Siloam fell on them—do you think they were more guilty than all the others living in Jerusalem? I tell you, no! But unless you repent, you too will all perish. (Lk.13:1-5)

Jesus was calling his contemporaries to repent of the constant rebellion against Rome that so characterized the Jewish nation. And he mourned over the coming disaster his people were about to experience:

> As he approached Jerusalem and saw the city, he wept over it and said, "If you, even you, had only known on this day what would bring you peace—but now it is hidden from your eyes. The days will come upon you when your enemies will build an embankment against you and encircle you and hem you in on every side. They will dash you to the ground, you and the children within your walls. They will not leave one stone on another, because you did not recognize the time of God's coming to you." (Lk.19:41-44)

Of course Jesus required his Jewish hearers in general to submit to the local Jewish authorities. He told the crowd: "The teachers of the law and the Pharisees sit in Moses' seat. So you must obey them and do everything they tell you," even though those leaders didn't practice what they preached (Mt.23:2, 3). So, even in regard to the local 'powers that be' whose lives were not to be imitated, Jesus required submission to their authority.

The next area in the life of a believer which Peter addressed was that of work. There was no equality in the Roman world between a slave and his or her master. Perhaps there were some benevolent Roman masters, but Peter didn't address a Christian slave's relationship with the benevolent master but with the harsh and unkind. Slavery was the basis of the Roman economy. Slaves were nothing more than property owned by their masters. A pagan master would have little sympathy for a Christian slave. It was to these Christian slaves that Peter wrote, but his instruction is valid for today also.

For most Christians in America, the nearest modern parallel to the slave/master relationship is that of employee/employer. How does one work for an overbearing employer? One does have the option today of resigning from such an unpleasant arrangement (that option was available also at times to slaves in the first century. See ICor.7:21). But, in the meantime, how should a believer conduct himself under adverse circumstances?

> Slaves, submit yourselves to your masters with all respect, not only to those who are good and considerate, but also to those who are harsh. For it is commendable if a man bears up under the pain of unjust suffering because he is conscious of God. But how is it to your credit if you receive a beating for doing wrong and endure it? But if you suffer for doing good and you endure it, this is commendable before God. To this you were called, because Christ suffered for you, leaving you an example, that you should follow in his steps. (IPet.2:18-21)

The third area of relationships Peter addressed was the home. Here also his language indicates inequality: wives were addressed with language which suggests they were married to unbelievers—Jewish or pagan:

> Wives, in the same way be submissive to your husbands so that, if any of them do not believe the word, they may be won over without words by the behavior of their wives, when

they see the purity and reverence of your lives. Your beauty should not come from outward adornment, such as braided hair and the wearing of gold jewelry and fine clothes. Instead, it should be that of your inner self, the unfading beauty of a gentle and quiet spirit, which is of great worth in God's sight. (3:1-4)

Any advice to husbands? Marriage in the first century A.D. was definitely patriarchal in nature. The husband was the unquestioned authority in the marriage relationship. So, the Christian husband, living in the 1st century culture, also had to learn a new way of relating to his wife. Christian husbands were instructed to be "considerate as you live with your wives, and treat them with respect as the weaker partner and as heirs with you of the gracious gift of life, so that nothing will hinder your prayers." (IPet.3:8)

But the question still remains: "How does one live in unequal relationships and suffer unjustly without losing one's joy?" We are told to follow Jesus' example, but Peter spoke only of what Jesus did, not how he did it. We are told Jesus had a certain attitude toward suffering, and that we should have the same attitude as we approach suffering: "Therefore, since Christ suffered in his body, arm yourselves with the same attitude." (IPet.4:1-2)

In order to uncover that attitude we must turn to the records of Jesus' life and see if we can discover his secret. We don't have to search long before we find it. Actually, it wasn't a secret at all; he lived it and taught it openly. Years after Jesus had ascended he revealed to Saul of Tarsus (now Paul, the persecuted) the basic principle of life: *"It is more blessed to give than to receive."* (Acts 20:35) Jesus lived and taught this: '*You learn how to live only when you learn how to give.*' You may find it incredulous that the basic principle of life should be reduced to learning how to give. How, then, does giving have any connection to "blessed are those who are persecuted for righteousness?"

First, perhaps proper giving has as much bearing on *avoiding* persecution as it does on *enduring* persecution. Peter urges his readers to "live such good lives among the pagans that, though they accuse you of doing wrong, they may see your good deeds and glorify God on the day he visits us." (IPet.212) And again, "For it is God's will that by doing good you should silence the ignorant talk of foolish men." (2:15) And again Peter urges:

But in your hearts set apart Christ as Lord. Always be prepared to give an answer to everyone who asks you to give the
reason for the hope that you have. But do this with gentleness
and respect, keeping a clear conscience, *so that those who
speak maliciously against your good behavior in Christ may be
ashamed of their slander."* (3:15,16, emphasis mine)

I am convinced it was the incredible giving of the early Christians which
caught the eye of the pagan world around them. When the pagans abandoned their sick, the Christians came in and, at the risk of their own lives,
cared for those ailing pagans. When the pagans abandoned their unwanted
infants, it was the followers of Jesus who sat patiently on the outskirts of
the cities and rescued those discarded infants. All of that counter-culture's
conduct toward those who had 'spoken maliciously against them' was a
direct result of their obeying Jesus' instruction on giving.

Jesus described two kinds of giving: One type of giving is the world's way
and brings unhappiness. Is it too broad a statement to say that all humans—Christian and non-Christian—are raised to give by the world's
standard? Certainly, a baby is born thinking only of its own needs, caring
not one whit that he wakes you up in the middle of the night if he's hungry
or thirsty. And unless a change is made in that thinking, the baby will go
through life to its grave operating off that self-centered standard. Jesus described that all-too-common lifestyle and clearly showed the futility of it:

If you love those who love you, what credit is that to you?
Even 'sinners' love those who love them. And if you do good
to those who are good to you, what credit is that to you? Even
'sinners' do that. And if you lend to those from whom you
expect repayment, what credit is that to you? Even 'sinners'
lend to 'sinners,' expecting to be repaid in full. (Lk.6:32-34)

You know the story. Stating it in the most rudimental terms, it is "You
scratch my back, and I'll scratch yours." It is giving with strings attached.
Such giving is rooted in our fallen nature that centers in our self. Christians
inadvertently encourage it even at Christmas time when we "*exchange
gifts."* And you know how you felt (and may still feel) if the gift you received was much less expensive and less desired than the one you gave. If
your happiness depends on receiving as much as you give, you will almost

always be unhappy. At least your life will be one giant roller coaster ride. You will have lost your joy. Jesus had a better way of giving:

The giving Jesus advocated and embodied brings life and joy:

> I tell you who hear me: Love your enemies, do good to those who hate you, bless those who curse you, pray for those who mistreat you. If someone strikes you on one cheek, turn to him the other also. If someone takes your cloak, do not stop him from taking your tunic. Give to everyone who asks you, and if anyone takes what belongs to you, do not demand it back. Do to others as you would have them do to you. (Lk.6:27)

> But love your enemies, do good to them, and lend to them without expecting to get anything back. Then your reward will be great, and you will be sons of the Most High, because he is kind to the ungrateful and wicked. Be merciful, just as your Father is merciful. (vv.35, 36)

This is not an easy task. I'm thinking of a woman some thirty years ago. She sat uneasily on the couch in my office. She had been urged many times by her Christian neighbors to come in and talk, but she repeatedly had refused. She wasn't a Christian, and her marriage was in serious trouble. It was evident she was at the end of her rope. Often she would be so frazzled she would run out of her house, jump into her car and drive off, leaving the children to fend for themselves. Her neighbors would go get the children and care for them until the woman calmed down. She had attempted suicide more than once.

Finally, she agreed to come talk. As we began the session I asked her to tell me about her situation. She started talking about her husband and how difficult it was living with him. From what she said, he must have been a real clod. Of course, from listening to counselees for years, I had mistakenly concluded that all men were clods—because the only ones who ever came for counseling were women who naturally told their side of the story. (Men seldom come asking for counsel for their troubled marriages. 'How can you improve on perfection!?')

So, she continued unloading her trash bag about their failing relationship.

Then, I made the mistake of saying, "I'll bet you give in to him a lot, don't you?" I shouldn't have asked. She opened another trash bag: "Give in? That's all I do is give in!" She had a long list of "giving ins." After a while, I stopped her. I said, "Look at me." She did. I said, "Don't you ever give in to your husband again!" Shocked, she asked, "What do you mean?" I replied, "Just what I said, 'Don't ever give in to your husband again.'" Then I added, "You must stop *giving in* to him and start *giving*." She was visibly shaken. A light seemed to turn on in her head—I could see it in her eyes. She said, "I don't know why I haven't thought of that before. I give to my friends all the time; I've just never thought of doing that to my husband."

I don't know the end of that story. She left the office saying, "I'm going to my husband's office and tell him right now." I remember thinking, "Oh Lord, please don't let him be in his office; he may suffer cardiac arrest."

Disciples of the Prince of Peace, however, do not run alone or without a path to follow. We are surrounded by a great cloud of witnesses and are urged to throw off every hindrance and to...

> ...fix our eyes on Jesus, the author and perfecter of our faith, who for the joy set before him endured the cross, scorning its shame, and sat down at the right hand of the throne of God. Consider him who endured such opposition from sinful men, so that you will not grow weary and lose heart. (Heb.12:2,3)

"Blessed are those who are persecuted for righteousness" translated into Relationship Language:

An expression (which must be an *unspoken* expression) covers most any relationship that is being threatened: *"I'll make allowance for your bad days."* Lives lived in close proximity will always be confronted by conflict and occasional dysfunctional conduct. Hermits have no such problems! But all who attempt to live in community suffer from a bad day occasionally—either causing it or suffering from others causing it. If relationships are to be stabilized and remain on an even keel, allowance must be made for those bad days.

Again, I say it must be *unspoken*. Neither words nor countenance must convey "Oh, I can see you are having another bad day; I'll make allowance for it again!" That only further estranges. Instead, make this beatitude "the shock absorber" of your life—choose to absorb, not retaliate or pass on hurts you have suffered. Make it the Rolaids or Tums of your life, absorbing the acid that comes your way from time to time. This approach to life, this manner of giving allows you to suffer unjustly without losing your joy.

When I was asked a few years ago to speak at a Christian university chapel, I was hesitant. I had spoken for years to students on hundreds of occasions and had always relished the opportunities. So, why was I hesitant on this occasion? Well, what would students sixty years younger than I be willing to hear from an old man? Seeing my reluctance, the one who invited me said, "Just tell them something you would like to have known when you were their age." When he suggested that, I said immediately, "I'll do it." I knew exactly what I would have loved to have known when I was their age. What I wouldn't have given to have heard someone tell me, "You learn how to live only when you learn how to give." Learning to "give expecting nothing in return" would have saved me many a heartache and disappointment. It would have enabled me to suffer unjustly without losing my joy. Jesus knew what he was talking about when he said, "Blessed are those who are persecuted for righteousness, for theirs is the kingdom of heaven." It really is more blessed to give than to receive!

This eighth beatitude concludes what might be considered the Introduction to the greatest sermon ever preached: the Sermon on the Mount. "He who has ears better listen." He who does listen and heed is like a man who built his house on the rock; when the storms of life threaten, his life will weather the storm, and he will have entered through the narrow gateway into eternal life.

PART TWO

Jesus' Stories of Grace

Introduction to Part Two

P ART TWO is a treatise on the grace of God as seen through the lens of Jesus' parables. I believe there is not only room but need for a book dealing with the subject of the grace of God, especially when seen through Jesus' parables.

I've cleared the table of leftovers from years of debate on the subject of grace—debated at times in an ungracious manner. Grace is the most defining doctrine of the Christian faith. It deserves the noblest presentation possible in order to convey the richness of the lavish feast God has in store for those who hunger for his grace. The parables of Jesus do just that.

Grace as concept or doctrine alone is a pale shadow of the reality of grace *experienced*. The parables allow us to experience grace vicariously through the lives of the characters Jesus created: a lost boy coming home to a father running to meet him, debts being erased, sins being forgiven, warnings against grace being rejected etc. Once we are exposed to these compelling stories, we are touched by the richness of the grace of God. Thus, this portion of the book presents the grace of God through story.

However, bear with me for a few chapters as I set the table for what I hope will be a nourishing meal, a cool drink of water satisfying the thirst for many travelers "weary and heavy laden" with burdens imagined to be lifted, but which still remain; hunger still not satisfied nor thirst quenched.

But be advised up front: this is not vegetarian or vegan fare; there's meat in these sayings of Jesus which, though nourishing once swallowed, should be chewed well before being ingested. Decide for yourself how it tastes!

SECTION I

"I will open my mouth in parables,

I will utter hidden things, things from old."

Ps. 78:2

"Jesus spoke all these things to the crowd in parables;

He did not say anything to them without using a parable."

Mt.13:34

Chapter 10

"Jesus' Use of Story"

I USED to say, upon referring to one of Jesus' stories, "This is *just* a parable." This dismissal of Jesus' stories revealed ignorance on my part. I must have thought, "Let's not spend a lot of time trying to search out the meaning of these figurative stories; let's get on to the solid stuff of propositional facts." I didn't say this openly because I didn't know that I didn't know the value of these epic stories. Had I been paying attention I would have known their value decades earlier. While still in David Lipscomb College, my long-time friend Bob Plunkett came to me one Sunday evening and reported what he had preached at the Bordeaux church that morning. It was the parable of the Unjust Steward. To this day, it is the only sermon I can remember from those early preaching days. Bob had discovered the value of Jesus' parables years before I. But I finally caught on. No longer do I ignorantly overlook them. Some of the most insightful perspectives on the kingdom of God are gained by looking through the windows Jesus opened by his stories.

Jesus was not the first Hebrew prophet to use parables as a teaching tool. In fact, parables were a common medium of communication throughout Jewish history. But, as far as we have record, no one used them as extensively or as exclusively as did Jesus. This was predicted in Ps.78:2—"I will open my mouth in parables; I will utter hidden things, things from of old." And sure enough, Matthew observed that Jesus, after a full day of teaching, had spoken "all these things to the crowd in parables; he did not say anything to them without using a parable." (Mt.13:34)

Jesus said nothing "without using a parable" may be hyperbole. But it is interesting to note that this method of teaching was so commonly used by Jesus it seems to have exasperated the Twelve. John's account of the last night before Jesus' arrest records that, after one of Jesus' more literal statements, the Twelve said, "Now you are speaking clearly and without using figures of speech." (Jn.16:29) His recorded parables are quite numerous: they total at least 53. How many others are not recorded, we don't know.

What is a parable? There are various derivative definitions: "a story within a story" or "an earthly story with a heavenly meaning." Basically, "parable" means 'something thrown along side something else.' We have adopted the Greek word παραβολή and use it freely in English: *parallel, paragraph, paramedic, paradigm,* and *paraphrase* to name just a few. From παραβολή we even get the root of our favorite sports: "to throw" and "ball."

Parables served Jesus' contemporaries much like radio served our grandparents. Radio provided our grandparents pictures inspired by words beamed over the airwaves. Unlike television, radio provided our grandparents no visuals—only words which created mental pictures. Jesus' words did the same. Jesus used words to paint on the minds of his hearers pictures of the kingdom of God. The Master Painter, using words, created masterpieces in the imaginations of his hearers. Those "paintings" are classics which have endured for two thousand years. They are not likely to fade any time soon.

Jesus used short parables and long parables. Most of the short parables were told in the early days of his ministry and had to do with general principles of the nature of the kingdom. Matthew chapter 13 comes to mind. It contains seven of these short parables, two of which are longer only because the disciples asked him to explain the parable, and Jesus obliged with a lengthy explanation.

The more lengthy parables occur toward the end of Jesus' ministry—in fact, most occur during the last week of his life (see Matthew chapters 21-25)—especially on the Tuesday before he was tried and executed. It was these parables which served as Jesus' indictments of the religious leaders and forced them to take extreme action: to subject him to an illegal trial and to execute him by the most cruel method known to man. These parables were aimed directly at the ruling authorities. Upon hearing them, the die was cast. Jesus must go. In the words of the high priest: "It is better that one man die than the whole nation perish." (Jn.11:49-50)

Most of these later, longer parables contain a unique quality. In them Jesus is both the story teller and the main character, and they spring up right on the spur of the moment, extemporaneously out of the brilliance of his mind as he was doing hand-to-hand combat with the forces that shortly were to kill him.

In all these Jesus was put on the spot and, 'right off the top of his head,' he created these memorable stories which increasingly endangered his life.

Before we turn to view some of his masterpieces, however, it will help us first to clear up an all-too-common misunderstanding of the kingdom. Communicating the nature of the kingdom was perhaps the most difficult teaching task that confronted Jesus and was the subject which occupied the majority of his teachings. His hearers had inherited hundreds of years of a deeply-engrained view of the kingdom as material and visible, having geographical boundaries, a standing army and a literal king sitting on an earthly throne. But Jesus came saying, "My kingdom is not of this world; if it were, my servants would fight...But now my kingdom is from another place." (Jn.18:36) Once, having been asked by the Pharisees when the kingdom of God would come, Jesus replied, "The kingdom of God does not come with your careful observation, nor will people say, 'Here it is,' or 'There it is,' because the kingdom of God is within you." (Lk.17:20-21) Jesus' own Twelve, after three years of instruction and just prior to his ascension, still asked, "Lord, are you at this time going to restore the kingdom to Israel?" (Acts 1:6)

Well, what is the kingdom? Very simply: It is God's reign in one's life. It is God's rule in the lives of people. Submission to God's rule in one's life is the kingdom power of which Jesus spoke. (See "Is the Church Interested in the Kingdom?" by Christian Smith, taken from *Voices Magazine*, July/ August, 1989). The fact that the church has often made the church its message rather than Christ and his kingdom may explain why many feel the church has no power and has lost its appeal.

Much of the early preaching I heard and did was concerned with describing the church. I don't remember ever hearing a sermon or reading an article differentiating between the kingdom and the church. This doesn't say there were none, but the distinct impression left on my young mind was that the church was the main message to be preached, and that church and kingdom were one and the same thing. Some even avoided reciting the Lord's Prayer, saying "How can we pray 'Thy kingdom come' since the kingdom came when the church was established on Pentecost?"

And you also may be thinking, "You mean the kingdom and the church are *not* one and the same thing?" No, they are not. The kingdom and the church definitely overlap, but the church is only the effect; the kingdom is the cause. The church is the light bulb; the kingdom is the electricity. The kingdom is the power that produces the church. The kingdom is the root; the church is the fruit. Whenever the kingdom is the message preached, the church is the visible result. Whenever the church is the message preached, a denomination is the visible result.

Unless a clear distinction between kingdom and church is understood (including the overlap), most of what Jesus taught will have little meaning, because most of Jesus' teaching had to do with the kingdom and the effect the kingdom has in the lives of his people—the church. Jesus had virtually no message but the kingdom. He spoke of the church twice (Matt.16:18 and 18:17). In Matthew alone it is recorded that he spoke of the kingdom 36 times and in Luke 45 times. Unless we preach the good news of the kingdom of God, we're not preaching the message Jesus preached nor the message he commissioned us to preach (Matt.28:19, 20; Mk.16:15,16). Even in the crucial days prior to his ascension, "He appeared to them over a period of forty days and spoke about the kingdom of God." (Acts 1:3) The Kingdom was his message and parables were his method.

No, I never say anymore, "This is *just* a parable." Anyone who has read the life of Jesus knows how many times he almost got killed over a story he told. Part of the power of a parable lies in the fact that the hearers are not aware of the message until the conclusion. By then it's too late; they've already taken the bait, the hook has been set and the hearers are caught.

I once was nearly mauled for telling a parable to a church in New Zealand. The background of the occasion was this: All the original missionaries had returned to the U.S., and the young church was left in the hands of the nationals. Soon there was grumbling against the local leaders to the point the church was in danger of imploding. John Payne (my coworker) and I went back to try to correct the problem. One Sunday morning I described a family which had lost both mother and father. Out of necessity the older brothers and sisters had to step in and do the cooking, etc. Well, the younger siblings began to grumble and complain about the food and the care they were getting. Then I looked the church in the eye and said, "You are that family."

Well, that did it; the fat was in the fire. One brother came over the benches ready to take me to task. I don't remember how I calmed him down, but I realized as he came toward me that a parable has the power to arouse to violence those convicted of its truth.

So, I no longer say, "This is *just* a parable." In fact, I now depend heavily on Jesus' parables because *he* depended heavily on them to put teeth into his teachings and to deliver the mysteries of the kingdom of God to those "who have ears to hear."

Chapter 11

"The Twos in the Story"

HAVE you ever noticed how many times in Jesus' parables he either uses the actual word "Two" or frames the story in juxtaposition: i.e., "placing two or more things together, especially in order to suggest a link between them or emphasize the contrast between them?" (Webster's Collegiate Dictionary) Juxtaposition is not totally equivalent to parable, but the two share some characteristics—especially in regard to Jesus' parables. Jesus was famous for framing his parables in such a fashion that, while showing a link between two subjects, he actually contrasted the two, setting them in juxtaposition.

Why would he do that? Mainly, because the kingdom he came to describe and to embody was diametrically opposite the kingdoms of earth. Jesus showed this contrast between the two when he said, "What is highly valued among men is detestable in God's sight" (Lk.16:15). Jesus used familiar figures but turned them up-side-down to get his hearers to start thinking differently.

It's no wonder, then, that Jesus' first recorded message was: "Repent." "Repent for the kingdom of heaven is near" (Mt.4:17). In calling us to repent, he implied that we possess the wrong one of two mindsets, and that we need to "change our mind"—notably, to the "mind of those who have begun to abhor their errors and misdeeds, and have determined to enter upon a better course of life…" (Thayer). There are only two minds, two roads, two gates; and Jesus urged his hearers to…

> …enter through the narrow gate. For wide is the gate and broad is the road that leads to destruction, and many enter through it. But small is the gate and narrow is the road that leads to life, and only a few find it." (Mt.7:13:14)

His life embodied that narrow way, and his stories described it.

Interestingly, the most glaring of these juxtapositions is found not in a parable but in statements which explain the difference between Jesus and us, thus justifying his practice of employing parables of contrast: "You are from below; I am from above. You are of this world; I am not of this world." (Jn.8:23) Because of this difference of origin, he came showing a contrast between the two—both by his life and his words.

He once drew a most startling contrast for those he fed on the eastern shore of Lake Galilee:

> Your forefathers ate the manna in the desert, yet they died. But here is the bread which comes down from heaven, which a man may eat and not die. I am the living bread that came down from heaven. If anyone eats of this bread, he will live forever. This bread is my flesh, which I will give for the life of the world." (Jn.6:49-51)

So it is only natural that in describing his kingdom he should use stories that posit one world against the other; one realm against the other, one bread against the other—himself being the only true bread of life—the one way, the one truth, the one life in contrast to any other bread, any other way, any other supposed truth or so-called life. He stands above and against them all.

Of course the rulers rejected his claims to the very end even though their objections were baseless at best and sheer nonsense at worst. One day Jesus was driving out a demon that was mute. "When the demon had left, the man who had been mute spoke, and the crowd was amazed."

> But some of them said, 'By Beelzebub, the prince of demons, he is driving out demons....' Jesus knew their thoughts and said, "Any kingdom divided against itself will be ruined, and a house divided against itself will fall. If Satan is divided against himself, how can his kingdom stand? But if I drive out demons by the finger of God, then the kingdom of God has come to you." (Lk.11:15-20)

So once again Jesus set out in bold contrast the difference between his way and ours; his kingdom and the world's. He does this in the story of a man who had two sons (Matt.21:28-32):

> What do you think? There was a man who had two sons. He went to the first and said, 'Son, go and work today in the vineyard.' 'I will not,' he answered, but later he changed his mind and went. Then the father went to the other son and said the same thing. He answered, 'I will, sir,' but he did not go. "Which of the two did what his father wanted?" "The first," they answered. Jesus said to them, "Truly I tell you, the tax collectors and the prostitutes are entering the kingdom of God ahead of you. For John came to you to show you the way of righteousness, and you did not believe him, but the tax collectors and the prostitutes did. And even after you saw this, you did not repent and believe him."

Another "two son" story is found in Luke 15:11-32 which we will examine closely in Chapters 14 and 15.

Still another of the "twos" is the story of the two debtors to which we alluded earlier but now quote in full. The setting was this: Jesus was a guest in Simon the Pharisee's house when a woman who had "lived a sinful life" came in and began touching Jesus (weeping, kissing and anointing his feet). Simon judged this as highly improper, to which Jesus replied, "Simon, I have something to tell you." "Tell me, Teacher," Simon said.

Two people owed money to a certain moneylender. One owed him five hundred denarii and the other fifty. Neither of them had the money to pay him back, so he forgave the debts of both. Now which of them will love him more?" Simon replied, "I suppose the one who had the bigger debt forgiven." "You have judged correctly," Jesus said. Then he turned toward the woman and said to Simon, "Do you see this woman? I came into your house. You did not give me any water for my feet, but she wet my feet with her tears and wiped them with her hair. You did not give me a kiss, but this woman, from the time I entered, has not stopped kissing my feet. You did not put oil on my head, but she has poured perfume on my feet. Therefore, I tell you, her many sins have been forgiven—as her great love has shown. But whoever has been forgiven little loves little. (Lk.7:36-47)

What a startling contrast Jesus drew with this parable. Simon as host should have provided the hospitable services: the welcoming kiss, the washing of feet, the traditional anointing with oil. He offered none of these usual amenities, whereas this woman who had crashed the party provided them all. What was the difference? Jesus' story explains: Simon, a strict, religious Pharisee felt little indebtedness to Jesus, whereas the woman who had been forgiven of great sins (evidently prior to her intrusion) felt overwhelming gratitude to Jesus for forgiving her many sins. She had been forgiven much and, consequently, loved much. Simon, who felt little need for forgiveness, loved little.

Though only a few parables actually use the word "two," many of Jesus' stories contain the theme of contrast between two parties or two subjects. For example: One of the most memorable is the story of the wise and foolish builders. We've sung about it from childhood. At the conclusion of what is called the Sermon on the Mount, Jesus said,

Therefore everyone who hears these words of mine and puts them into practice is like a wise man who built his house on the rock. The rain came down, the streams rose, and the winds blew and beat against that house; yet it did not fall, because it had its foundation on the rock. But everyone who hears these words of mine and does not put them into practice is like a foolish man who built his house on sand. The rain came down, the streams rose, and the winds blew and beat against that house, and it fell with a great crash. (Mt.7:24-27)

Most people build their lives on sand and suffer the consequences. Those who build on the rock reap the rewards of a successful life. From the very start of Jesus' ministry he made this crystal clear by contrasting the two, calling us to build our lives not on sand but on the solid rock of his teachings. 'The proof of the building is in the standing thereof.'

The following list of parables built on the theme of juxtaposition does not claim to be exhaustive or even completely accurate, since some of the parables overlap their assigned categories. The list is representative of the underlying theme of juxtaposition or contrast. In my research I have not found any parable based on simple comparison; they all are constructed along the line of contrast. The categories I have chosen to represent these stories of contrast are:

1) Parables which feature "Things" (inanimate or non-human characters).

2) Parables which feature "Groups" of people as the characters.

3) Parables which feature "Individuals" as the main character.

Parables Featuring "Things"

MANY of Jesus' early parables featured inanimate and non-human objects: salt, soils, rocks, thorns, good seeds, bad seeds, small seeds, pearls, yeast, coins, sheep, cloth, wineskins, wine, fish, nets, trees, bushels, bowls, beds, banquets and hidden treasures. In this category featuring "things," the overlap of categories is obvious because each of these things is connected to the transition which occurs when the seed of the kingdom is planted in the hearts of human beings.

Also, this whole category overlaps with the third category in which we address the "progression" of story evident in the unfolding drama of Jesus' life. The progression advances from the simple to the complex, from the figurative to the literal, from general didactic to specific accusations of condemnation; escalating from the innocuous to the very dangerous, leading eventually to his arrest, trial and crucifixion.

Those early, short, general parables employing non-human objects described mainly the nature of the kingdom and were completely inoffensive. The two earliest parables were perhaps Jesus' simplest: One story in Mt.5:13 simply drew a distinction between active and inactive salt. Active salt performs its unique work of preservation, while salt that has lost it saltiness is "no longer good for anything except to be thrown out and trampled by men."

The other is in Mt.5:14-16:

> You are the light of the world. A town built on a hill cannot be hidden. Neither do people light a lamp and put it under a bowl. Instead they put it on its stand, and it gives light to everyone in the house. In the same way, let your light shine before others, that they may see your good deeds and glorify your Father in heaven.

As we have noted above, the early, short, general parables are most tightly grouped in Matthew chapter 13. (There are parallels in Mark and Luke.) Matthew opens the 13th chapter describing a day in Jesus' life:

> That same day Jesus went out of the house and sat by the lake. Such large crowds gathered around him that he got into a boat and sat in it, while all the people stood on the shore. Then he told them many things in parables, saying: "A farmer went out to sow his seed. As he was scattering the seed, some fell along the path, and the birds came and ate it up. Some fell on rocky places, where it did not have much soil. It sprang up quickly, because the soil was shallow. But when the sun came up, the plants were scorched, and they withered because they had no root. Other seed fell among thorns, which grew up and choked the plants. Still other seed fell on good soil, where it produced a crop—a hundred, sixty or thirty times what was sown. (13:1-9)

Then Jesus added this oft-repeated admonition: "Whoever has ears, let him hear." (Mt.13:1-9) The Net Bible translates that admonition in this way: "The one who has ears had better listen."

Jesus told them another parable:

> The kingdom of heaven is like a man who sowed good
> seed in his field. But while everyone was sleeping, his en-
> emy came and sowed weeds among the wheat, and went
> away. When the wheat sprouted and formed heads, then the
> weeds also appeared. "The owner's servants came to him
> and said, 'Sir, didn't you sow good seed in your field? Where
> then did the weeds come from?' 'An enemy did this,' he re-
> plied. The servants asked him, 'Do you want us to go and
> pull them up?' 'No,' he answered, 'because while you are
> pulling the weeds, you may uproot the wheat with them.
> Let both grow together until the harvest. At that time I will
> tell the harvesters: First collect the weeds and tie them in
> bundles to be burned; then gather the wheat and bring it
> into my barn.' (13:24-30)

He told them still another parable in which the contrast lay simply in the
"before and after" effects of the kingdom:

> The kingdom of heaven is like a mustard seed, which a man
> took and planted in his field. Though it is the smallest of all
> seeds, yet when it grows, it is the largest of garden plants
> and becomes a tree, so that the birds come and perch in its
> branches. (13:31, 32)

Still another parable showed the "before and after:" "The kingdom of heav-
en is like yeast that a woman took and mixed into a large amount of flour
until it worked all through the dough." (13:33)

Two more parables in this 13th chapter emphasize—again by contrast:

1)   The inestimable value of the kingdom over any prized possession:

> The kingdom of heaven is like treasure hidden in a field.
> When a man found it, he hid it again, and then in his joy
> went and sold all he had and bought that field. Again, the
> kingdom of heaven is like a merchant looking for fine pearls.

When he found one of great value, he went away and sold everything he had and bought it. (13:44-46)

2) The separation of good from evil at the final Judgment:

> ... the kingdom of heaven is like a net that was let down into the lake and caught all kinds of fish. When it was full, the fishermen pulled it up on the shore. Then they sat down and collected the good fish in baskets, but threw the bad away. This is how it will be at the end of the age. The angels will come and separate the wicked from the righteous and throw them into the blazing furnace, where there will be weeping and gnashing of teeth. (13:47-50)

Jesus ended this lengthy teaching session by asking his disciples if they had understood "all these things." They answered, "Yes." In fact, I doubt they did. (Can you think of a time when they *ever* understood what Jesus said?) But Jesus didn't take issue with them. He simply concluded by saying, "Therefore every teacher of the law who has become a disciple in the kingdom of heaven is like the owner of a house who brings out of his storeroom new treasures as well as old." (Mt.13:52)

"New as well as old." People who are disciples of the kingdom of heaven will be a flexible, balanced people, bringing out of their treasure things "new and old." Without this flexibility and balance, they will be like a person who sews a piece of unshrunk cloth onto an old garment: a greater tear is made (Mt.9:16). Or one who pours new wine into old wineskins: the new wine will burst the skins, and the wine will be spilled. "No," said Jesus, "They pour new wine into new wineskins and both are preserved." (Mt.9:17)

The above listing is not exhaustive; it gives only a general idea of the nature of Jesus' early parables. They were simple, basic principles of the kingdom of God. They were spoken in the simplest of language, using terms familiar to his hearers. Such is the nature of Jesus' early parables describing the kingdom at its most basic level.

We turn now to address the more complex parables.

Parables Featuring Groups

AS Jesus' hearers began to grasp—or fail to grasp—what he was saying, they began to form opinions about him—both positive and negative, and thus opinion *groups* began to develop. Jesus knew this would happen:

> Do not suppose that I have come to bring peace to the earth. I did not come to bring peace, but a sword. For I have come to turn a man against his father, a daughter against her mother, a daughter-in-law against her mother-in-law—a man's enemies will be those of his own household. (Mt.10:36-38)

Micah (7:6) had prophesied this, and Jesus had predicted it. John, in particular, makes specific reference to this formation of opinion groups:

> Among the crowds there was widespread whispering about him. Some said, "He is a good man." Others replied, "No, he deceives the people." (Jn.7:12)

> On hearing his words, some of the people said, "Surely this man is the Prophet." Others said, "He is the Messiah." Still others asked, "How can the Messiah come from Galilee? Does not Scripture say that the Messiah will come from David's descendants and from Bethlehem, the town where David lived?" Thus the people were divided because of Jesus. Some wanted to seize him, but no one laid a hand on him. (Jn.7:40-44)

> At these words the Jews were again divided. Many of them said, "He is demon-possessed and raving mad. Why listen to him?" But others said, "These are not the words of a man possessed of a demon." (Jn.10:19-21)

So, the opinion groups were forming and, according to the Synoptic Gospels, the parables were a major part of the cause. For example: after telling the parable of the soils (Lk.8:5-8), Jesus' disciples came to him and asked him what this parable meant. He responded by saying,

> The knowledge of the secrets of the kingdom of God has been given to you, but to others I speak in parables so that

though seeing, they may not see; though hearing, they may not understand. (8:10)

Unquestionably, Jesus made a clear distinction between the "disciples" group and the group of "others"—even though the disciples didn't understand the meaning of the parable either. This distinction seems to have had little to do with the disciples (as a group) having keener insight than the "others." Jesus had his own reasons for selecting the Twelve. It seems to have been predicated only on Jesus' choice of disciples to whom he would entrust the "knowledge of the secrets of the kingdom of God." He imparted this knowledge by explaining these parables to them but not to the "others."

Yet, Mark records, "With many similar parables Jesus spoke the word to [the crowd], *as much as they could understand*. He did not say anything to them without using a parable. But when he was alone with his disciples, *he explained everything*." (Mk.4:33, 34) There seems, therefore, to have been more than one level of understanding among those who heard the parables. This shouldn't surprise us as we note the different levels of understanding that currently exist universally in every field of knowledge. In the case of understanding the parables, Jesus chose to reveal the deeper truths of the kingdom to the group he had chosen—the Twelve.

With this perhaps inadequate explanation, let us look at some of those "Parables Featuring Groups." Here again, the categories bleed over into each other. Simultaneously, a particular parable may revolve around an individual but also involve others as a group. For example:

Luke records in the 14th chapter several interesting conversations Jesus had with the dinner guests in the home of a "prominent Pharisee." The meal didn't begin in a very congenial manner: Jesus "was being carefully watched." (14:1)

> There in front of him was a man suffering from dropsy. Jesus asked the Pharisees and experts in the law, "Is it lawful to heal on the Sabbath or not?" But they remained silent. So, taking hold of the man, he healed him and sent him away. (14:2-4)

To prove his point, Jesus then asked them, "If one of you has a son or an ox that falls into a well on the Sabbath day, will you not immediately pull him out?" And they had nothing to say (14:5, 6).

Having dealt with the thorny subject of Sabbath activity, Jesus turned his attention to—would you believe—social graces. He must have arrived early for the dinner because he was able to watch the other guests as they arrived:

> When he noticed how the guests picked the places of honor at the table, he told them this parable: "When someone invites you to a wedding feast, do not take the place of honor, for a person more distinguished than you may have been invited. If so, the host who invited both of you will come and say to you, 'Give this person your seat.' Then, humiliated, you will have to take the least important place. But when you are invited, take the lowest place, so that when your host comes, he will say to you, 'Friend, move up to a better place.' Then you will be honored in the presence of all the other guests. For all those who exalt themselves will be humbled, and those who humble themselves will be exalted. (14:7-11)

When he saw the kind of guests who were arriving, he advised the host:

> When you give a luncheon or dinner, do not invite your friends, your brothers or sisters, your relatives, or your rich neighbors; if you do, they may invite you back and so you will be repaid. But when you give a banquet, invite the poor, the crippled, the lame, the blind, and you will be blessed. Although they cannot repay you, you will be repaid at the resurrection of the righteous. (14:12-14)

When one of the guests heard this advice, he exclaimed: "Blessed is the man who will eat at the feast in the kingdom of God." (v. 15) Jesus replied with a parable in which the invited guests simply asked to be excused. Though the host was "angry," the only retribution was that those who had excused themselves were granted their wish: they didn't get a taste of the banquet.

> A certain man was preparing a great banquet and invited many guests. At the time of the banquet he sent his servant to

tell those who had been invited, 'Come, for everything is now ready.' But they all alike began to make excuses. The first said, 'I have just bought a field, and I must go and see it. Please excuse me.' Another said, 'I have just bought five yoke of oxen, and I'm on my way to try them out. Please excuse me.' Still another said, 'I just got married, so I can't come.' (14:16-20)

The servant came back and reported this to his master. Then the owner of the house became angry and ordered his servant, 'Go out quickly into the streets and alleys of the town and bring in the poor, the crippled, the blind and the lame.' 'Sir,' the servant said, 'what you ordered has been done, but there is still room.' Then the master told his servant, 'Go out to the roads and country lanes and compel them to come in, so that my house will be full. I tell you, not one of those who were invited will get a taste of my banquet.' (14:21-24)

Jesus pictured another group of critics as children playing:

To what can I compare this generation? They are like children sitting in the market places and calling out to others: 'We played the flute for you, and you did not dance; we sang a dirge, and you did not mourn.' (Mt.11:16, 17)

In other words, that generation couldn't be satisfied regardless what was offered them, for "John came neither eating nor drinking, and they say, 'He has a demon.' The Son of Man came eating and drinking, and they say, 'Here is a glutton and a drunkard; a friend of tax collectors and sinners.'" (Mt.11:18, 19)

Two very prominent "group" parables complete this category. First:

At that time the kingdom of heaven will be like ten virgins who took their lamps and went out to meet the bridegroom. Five of them were foolish and five were wise. The foolish ones took their lamps but did not take any oil with them. The wise ones, however, took oil in jars along with their lamps. The bridegroom was a long time in coming, and they all became drowsy and fell asleep.

At midnight the cry rang out: 'Here's the bridegroom! Come out to meet him!' Then all the virgins woke up and trimmed their lamps. The foolish ones said to the wise, 'Give us some of your oil; our lamps are going out.' 'No,' they replied, 'there may not be enough for both us and you. Instead, go to those who sell oil and buy some for yourselves.'

But while they were on their way to buy the oil, the bridegroom arrived. The virgins who were ready went in with him to the wedding banquet. And the door was shut. "Later the others also came. 'Lord, Lord,' they said, 'open the door for us!' But he replied, 'Truly I tell you, I don't know you.' (Mt.25:1-12)

"Therefore keep watch," Jesus said, "because you do not know the day or the hour." (25:13)

The second is the broadest "group" parable of all, since "all of the nations of the world" will be gathered before him and will be separated into two groups:

When the Son of Man comes in his glory, and all the angels with him, he will sit on his glorious throne. All the nations will be gathered before him, and he will separate the people one from another as a shepherd separates the sheep from the goats. He will put the sheep on his right and the goats on his left.

Then the King will say to those on his right, 'Come, you who are blessed by my Father; take your inheritance, the kingdom prepared for you since the creation of the world. For I was hungry and you gave me something to eat, I was thirsty and you gave me something to drink, I was a stranger and you invited me in, I needed clothes and you clothed me, I was sick and you looked after me, I was in prison and you came to visit me.'

Then the righteous will answer him, 'Lord, when did we see you hungry and feed you, or thirsty and give you something to drink? When did we see you a stranger and invite you in, or needing clothes and clothe you? 'When did we see you sick or in prison and go to visit you?' The King will reply, 'Truly I tell you, whatever you did for one of the least of these brothers and sisters of mine, you did for me.'

Then he will say to those on his left, 'Depart from me, you who are cursed, into the eternal fire prepared for the devil and his angels. For I was hungry and you gave me nothing to eat, I was thirsty and you gave me nothing to drink, I was a stranger and you did not invite me in, I needed clothes and you did not clothe me, I was sick and in prison and you did not look after me.'

They also will answer, 'Lord, when did we see you hungry or thirsty or a stranger or needing clothes or sick or in prison, and did not help you?' He will reply, 'Truly I tell you, whatever you did not do for one of the least of these, you did not do for me.' Then they will go away to eternal punishment, but the righteous to eternal life. (Mt.25:31-46)

This final scene, dividing the people of all nations into two groups, is both sobering and simplifying. It is sobering in that it speaks of "eternal punishment" and "eternal life." There is a finality in these two expressions which sobers us and makes us realize that while we are living we are deciding which group we will be in as we stand before the Great Judgment Throne. It is interesting to note that neither group was aware of having seen Jesus in any of the needy conditions he mentions. Neither group was aware of the implications of their earthly actions: "Lord, when did we see you…"

It is simplifying in that it makes the litmus test of acceptance before God not a complicated, extended hair-splitting theology requiring great knowledge and understanding. This picture of the final judgment—the "final exam"—is simply "How did I treat others when I met them along the way?" "Was I kind and generous to the hungry, the thirsty, the naked, the sick, those in prison, etc.?" "Did I recognize Jesus in those needy people?" Those who preach what is called a "social gospel" emphasize this judgment scene (and rightly so) but ignore a very subtle implication in the story: This scene involves people—all of whom recognize Jesus as *Lord*. Both groups ask, "*Lord*, when did we see you hungry or thirsty or a stranger..."

Perhaps it is only after "every knee had bowed and every tongue confessed Jesus as Lord" that both sheep and goats of all the nations call him "Lord." This view would give the balance we find throughout Jesus' ministry and in the subsequent writings of his disciples. There is no question that Jesus required other specifics as necessary to discipleship—such as his forthright statement to Nicodemus: "No one can see the kingdom of God unless he is born again....born of water and the Spirit." (Jn. 3:3, 5) "Unless you believe that I am the one I claim to be, you will indeed die in your sins." (Jn. 8:24) "Unless you change and become like little children, you will never enter the kingdom of heaven." (Mt.18:2) And his unequivocal call to "love each other" saying, "By this all men will know that you are my disciples." (Jn.13:35) So, Jesus made many specific requirements for discipleship.

But could it be that all the specific requirements Jesus makes on his disciples come down in the final analysis to this test: "How did I, in Jesus' name, treat people while I was living on earth?" A further thought adds weight to this conclusion. Jesus' cousin John described the requirements of the kingdom in a similar way. He came preparing the way for Jesus. He came preaching the good news of the kingdom, preaching a "baptism of repentance for the remission of sins." (Lk.3:3) But, further, he called them to "produce fruit worthy of repentance." (3:8) Upon hearing and accepting this call, the crowd asked, "What then should we do?" To this, John answered:

> "Anyone who has two shirts should share with the one who has none, and anyone who has food should do the same." Even tax collectors came to be baptized. "Teacher," they asked, "what should we do?" "Don't collect any more than you are required to," he told them. Then some soldiers asked him, "And what should we do?" He replied, "Don't extort money and don't accuse people falsely—be content with your pay." (Lk.3:11-14)

Notice: In both John's introductory description of the kingdom and its fruit (Lk.3:1-14) and Jesus' final scene of the kingdom (Matt.25:31-46), the emphasis is the same: "How did we treat people" (specifically as related to their physical needs). I wonder if this is the bottom line of "You shall love the Lord your God…and "you shall love your neighbor as you love yourself." John the apostle suggests this very relationship: "If anyone has material possessions and sees his brother in need and has no pity on him, how can the love of God be in him?" (IJn.3:17)

There is the familiar story of a man to whom the Lord appeared in a dream promising to visit him the next day. The man excitedly cleaned his house and made special preparations to host the Lord. During his preparations there was a knock at the door. There stood a widow asking for assistance, but he told her he didn't have time to help her; he was involved in something very important. He closed the door and continued preparing for the Lord. There was another knock, and there stood a barefooted orphan asking for shoes. The man declined, closed the door and continued preparing to host the Lord. A third knock came; this time it was a beggar asking for food. Not having time to stop and prepare the food, he dismissed the beggar.

That night the Lord appeared again in a dream. The man expressed his disappointment: "I prepared, but you never came." The Lord replied, "I came three times, but you never let me in."

I wonder how many times our Lord has visited us, and we didn't recognize him! So, he warns, "Be on guard, for you do not know the day or the hour." (Mt. 25:13)

Parables Featuring Individuals

WE turn now to parables featuring individuals. This change of venue is consistent with Jesus' attempt to emphasize the requirements of discipleship and the individual responsibilities of stewardship. Either the story was triggered by an individual, or the story is built around an individual. It is the latter of these two which interests us as we consider the contrasting nature of the "Two" parables. We have already referred above to one of the most memorable "Two" theme parables—the wise and foolish builders. (Mt.7:24-27) The "Unmerciful Servant" will be examined in depth in chapter 17.

The "Two" theme of contrast emerges in yet another servant parable, as Jesus contrasts two possible scenarios in one servant. Jesus tells the parable as a warning against slothful servanthood, because "the Son of Man will come at an hour when you do not expect him."

> Who then is the faithful and wise servant, whom the master has put in charge of the servants in his household to give them their food at the proper time? It will be good for that servant whose master finds him doing so when he returns. Truly I tell you, he will put him in charge of all his possessions. But suppose that servant is wicked and says to himself, 'My master is staying away a long time,' and he then begins to beat his fellow servants and to eat and drink with drunkards. The master of that servant will come on a day when he does not expect him and at an hour he is not aware of. He will cut him to pieces and assign him a place with the hypocrites, where there will be weeping and gnashing of teeth. (Mt.23:45-51)

Another wise and foolish servant theme is found in Matthew's gospel (Mt.25:14-30) with a variant account in Luke 19:11-27. These two parables emphasize the theme of responsible stewardship. Though there are three servants, not just two, Jesus highlights the two contrasting attitudes.

> Again, it will be like a man going on a journey who called his servants and entrusted his wealth to them. To one he gave five bags of gold, to another two bags, and to another one bag each according to his ability. Then he went on his journey. The man who had received five bags of gold went at once and put his money to work and gained five bags more. So also, the one with two bags of gold gained two more. But the man who had received one bag went off, dug a hole in the ground and hid his master's money.
>
> After a long time the master of those servants returned and settled accounts with them. The man who had received five bags of gold brought the other five. 'Master,' he said, 'you entrusted me with five bags of gold. See, I have gained five more.' His master replied, 'Well done, good and faithful servant! You have been faithful with a few things; I will put you in charge of many things. Come and share your master's happiness!'

The man with two bags of gold also came. 'Master,' he said, 'you entrusted me with two bags of gold; see, I have gained two more.' His master replied, 'Well done, good and faithful servant! You have been faithful with a few things; I will put you in charge of many things. Come and share your master's happiness!'

Then the man who had received one bag of gold came. 'Master,' he said, 'I knew that you are a hard man, harvesting where you have not sown and gathering where you have not scattered seed. So I was afraid and went out and hid your gold in the ground. See, here is what belongs to you.' His master replied, 'You wicked, lazy servant! So you knew that I harvest where I have not sown and gather where I have not scattered seed? Well then, you should have put my money on deposit with the bankers, so that when I returned I would have received it back with interest. So take the bag of gold from him and give it to the one who has ten bags. For whoever has will be given more, and they will have an abundance. Whoever does not have, even what they have will be taken from them. And throw that worthless servant outside, into the darkness, where there will be weeping and gnashing of teeth. (Mat.25:14-30)

Interestingly, in the totally unique parable of the "shrewd manager" (Lk.16:1-13), there are more contrasts than in any other parable: 1) honesty vs dishonesty; 2) employed vs unemployed; 3) digging vs begging; 4) true vs false billing; 5) Jesus' statements re: worldly wealth and eternal dwellings; 6) little vs much; 7) worldly wealth vs true riches; 8) other's property vs your own; 9) "No servant can serve two masters." Then, 10) Jesus flatly says, "You cannot serve both God and Money."

"The Pharisees, who loved money, heard all this and were sneering at Jesus." He said to them, "You are the ones who justify yourselves in the eyes of men, but God knows your hearts. What is highly valued among men is detestable in God's sight." (Lk.16:14, 15)

Dropping down to verse 19 we see once again the theme of contrast in the parable of the rich man and Lazarus—a classic by any measure:

There was a rich man who was dressed in purple and fine linen and lived in luxury every day. At his gate was laid a beggar named Lazarus, covered with sores and longing to eat what fell from the rich man's table. Even the dogs came and licked his sores.

The time came when the beggar died and the angels carried him to Abraham's side. The rich man also died and was buried. In Hades, where he was in torment, he looked up and saw Abraham far away, with Lazarus by his side. So he called to him, 'Father Abraham, have pity on me and send Lazarus to dip the tip of his finger in water and cool my tongue, because I am in agony in this fire.'

But Abraham replied, 'Son, remember that in your lifetime you received your good things, while Lazarus received bad things, but now he is comforted here and you are in agony. And besides all this, between us and you a great chasm has been set in place, so that those who want to go from here to you cannot, nor can anyone cross over from there to us.'

He answered, 'Then I beg you, father, send Lazarus to my family, for I have five brothers. Let him warn them, so that they will not also come to this place of torment.' Abraham replied, 'They have Moses and the Prophets; let them listen to them.' 'No, father Abraham,' he said, 'but if someone from the dead goes to them, they will repent.' He said to him, 'If they do not listen to Moses and the Prophets, they will not be convinced even if someone rises from the dead.' (Lk.16:19-31)

Two other less visible stories which definitely point up the theme of contrast are found in Matthew 20:40 and 41. "At the coming of the Son of Man, two men will be in the field; one will be taken and the other left. Two women will be grinding with a hand mill; one will be taken and the other left." These two short parables have become the basis of the popular but highly speculative "Left Behind" series of novels by Tim LaHaye and Jerry Jenkins.

Then, of course, there is the classic "Pharisee and Tax Collector" parable showing in very few words the stark contrast between pride and humility:

To some who were confident of their own righteousness and looked down on everyone else, Jesus told this parable: "Two men went up to the temple to pray, one a Pharisee and the other a tax collector. The Pharisee stood by himself and prayed: 'God, I thank you that I am not like other people—robbers, evildoers, adulterers—or even like this tax collector. I fast twice a week and give a tenth of all I get.'

But the tax collector stood at a distance. He would not even look up to heaven, but beat his breast and said, 'God, have mercy on me, a sinner.'

I tell you that this man, rather than the other, went home justified before God. For all those who exalt themselves will be humbled, and those who humble themselves will be exalted. (Lk.18:9-14)

The "Two" theme runs throughout the records of the life and ministry of Jesus. I found other instances among which there were two fish, two angels, two blind men, two thieves crucified, two hands, two feet, two eyes, two witnesses, two disciples, two commandments, two days, two by two, a pair of turtle doves or two young pigeons, two boats, two coats, two men (Moses and Elijah), two silver coins, two pennies, two mites, two swords. Most of these were not parables, and most of these were not set in juxtaposition or contrast, but it is interesting how large a part the number "two" plays in the ministry of Jesus.

Chapter 12

"Jesus' Place in the Story"

WHILE attending a missionary retreat in Kenya several years ago, a missionary took me aside and asked, "May I speak with you for a few minutes?" I said, "Of course." So we sat down, and he began to tell his story. "I've been in Africa sixteen years," he said. "I came shortly after I preached a sermon on grace. I was fired...and here I am." I asked him to tell me about his sermon, which he did. As he spoke I saw something in him, in myself and in the subject of God's grace I had not seen before.

After listening to his story, I said, "I know why you were fired for preaching on grace: you preached on grace as though it were a theological doctrine. As you talked, I realized I had been preaching on grace for many years without being aware of it." I said, "Whereas you preached on grace as a theological doctrine, I preached on grace as a Person, and I never got fired."

Perhaps the church didn't realize what I was doing any more than I did. I know one thing: the church loved what they heard, for grace is good news! My feet aren't all that beautiful—with one exception: "How beautiful are the feet of those who bring good news." (Rom.10:15) "Grace is good news!"

Preaching grace today in the 21st Century (even as a theological doctrine) is not likely to produce throughout the church the same discomfort it did fifty years ago. I'm thankful that now in most churches we can preach as well as sing about grace. In fact, someone has observed, "If we would preach what we sing we would be pretty doctrinally sound." Like the country singer Mel Tillis: he normally stuttered while speaking. but when he started singing his speech impediment disappeared. We sing a wonderfully full and clear gospel. Don't you agree that, if we lived and preached fully what we sing, the impediments in our message to the world would fairly well disappear?

In order to enjoy the full benefits of grace, the subject must be understood not just academically or theologically. It must be understood emotionally and experientially—which is what happens as one listens to Jesus' parables. Jesus' parables are the melodies that carry the lyrics of God's grace into our hearts. We need the music of the parables!

When one understands Jesus' parables, two powerful results occur:

Firstly: We are enabled to accept our own inadequate and never complete pursuit of holiness, realizing that we are not saved by our own works of righteousness but by the grace of God. The only holiness we have is what is bestowed on us by the grace of God. It allows us to remove our masks and just be ourselves while God is transforming us into his likeness. And,

Secondly: It rescues us from judgmentalism. It allows us, indeed requires us, to get off other peoples' backs who happen to be different from us, thus saving us from divisiveness among ourselves and from elitism which separates us from those who are not "one of us." It allows us to come to the table with other imperfect believers and pursue unity and peace.

Both of these benefits are good news, wonderfully good news.

But there is also some sad news to report: Most people live outside the realm of grace. And sadder still is the fact that many Christians live outside the grace of God. But, how can this possibly be? Well, in the first place, two thirds of the world don't know Christ and don't own him as Lord, the God of grace. For instance, twenty-three percent (1.57 billion) of the world's population are Muslims. The Muslim religion knows nothing about the grace of God. Add to that the other major world religions (Hindu, Buddhist, Taoism, Satanism, Atheism etc.—all part of the 4,200 total religions in the world), and we begin to see the picture.

And in the second place, when one considers the largest contingent of professed Christians on earth—the Roman Catholic Church (numbering in excess of one billion)—which has historically championed salvation by works, not grace—the picture becomes even clearer: *most people on earth live outside the realm of God's grace.* At the very least, most live outside an *awareness* of God's grace.

The statistical numbering of religions, however, is not what I refer to when I say "Many Christians live their lives outside the grace of God." I refer instead to those who know God's grace theoretically but not experientially. No doubt many believers in God have heard of the grace of God in some form or other yet have not accessed it emotionally or experientially. For all practical purposes, (using current computer terminology) they have not "logged on" to grace, even though they live in the age of grace—much like many people who live in the world of computers but have not, themselves, "logged on" to the World Wide Web. They live in the midst of the WWW but lack the benefits of it.

I have two sisters. Bettye, the older of two, has been virtually all her life an avid writer of letters. It began after she met an invalid neighbor girl in Winchester, Tennessee. Bettye was twelve years old. Every afternoon after school she would go next door and visit Ann Halliburton—born totally spastic and unable to care for herself. They became hard, fast friends. When we moved from Winchester, Bettye wrote Ann twice a week for 30 years (that's 3,120 letters)! In addition to that, after Ann's death, Bettye continued to write Ann's mother until she also died.

As time passed, the world changed. Computers were invented, and email became the popular means of written communication. Bettye's family urged her to upgrade her method of correspondence. She declined: "Email? No thank you; it's too complicated for one 76 years old." But she finally agreed with Jodi, the younger sister: "If an email thingy can be bought for less than $100, I'll try it." Eventually Jodi found one advertised for $99.99. She bought it, installed the software, drove to Shelbyville, TN, stood as a warm body beside Bettye and started from scratch. "Turn on that switch," etc.

And it worked. Thus, thanks to Jodi, Bettye began to enjoy the World Wide Web. Jodi did all the hard work—Bettye just enjoyed the benefits.

"But," you may be asking, "How do I log on to grace?" Well, it's not all that easy for an older generation since we're not "grace literate." We are more likely to be "works literate." We prefer to get our righteousness the old fashioned way: Earn it! Grace is not our native tongue. But, if someone could stand beside us and walk us through it, we might be willing to try. We ask: "Are you sure we don't have to read some thick installation manual and understand a lot of theology and churcheze?" That's right. In Jesus we have a warm body who did all the hard work—we just enjoy the benefits.

It's somewhat like the time my wife Louine and I and our three sons, having completed our work in New Zealand, decided to go on around the world via Europe. We ordered a Volkswagen camper and had it shipped from Germany to Haifa, Israel to serve as our means of transportation through Europe. While waiting to depart New Zealand, I bought language books for five different European countries. We learned how to ask the very basic questions: "Where is the WC?" "How do you get to the Coliseum?" "Where …," on and on. Each of us took a language. We studied hard and quizzed each other on these basic questions regularly over the next several weeks.

We put the two younger siblings—Amy and Rachel—on a plane (with a special stewardess) to their Granny in Tennessee. We then flew out of Christchurch, NZ in March, 1970 all prepared to wind our way for three months through unknown territory—especially unknown languages. But we had studied hard and knew how to ask the basic questions. So off we went.

It wasn't until we got to Madrid, Spain that we had a rude awakening. We wanted to go see the arena where the bull fights took place. Spanish was our youngest son Jon's assigned language. Now was his big chance to display his language skills. We saw a friendly-looking lady waiting to cross the street in downtown Madrid. We drove up to her; Jon rolled down his window and in his best Spanish asked the lady, "Which way to the stadium of the bulls?" His question must have been asked in impeccable Spanish because that dear lady started rattling off in *Spanish* the directions to the stadium where the bull fights occur. Not until that moment did we realize that, though we could ask the question, *we couldn't understand the answer!*

We just turned and looked at each other in stunned amazement and broke out laughing. We hadn't a clue what she said.

That's similar to our trying to understand grace: We know how to ask the question but, since grace is not our native language, we don't know how to understand the answer. We sit scratching our heads, wanting to get to grace but not understanding how.

Well, the rest of the bull story may help make the application clear. When the lady in Madrid saw the look on our faces, she said (in English), "Let me get in your car, and I'll show you the way to the arena." Talk about good news!! She got in, and in no time we were sitting in front of the arena.

That's what Jesus did for us when "The Word became flesh and dwelt among us." He 'got in our car' and rode with us, showing and telling us (in our native language) about the grace of God. "We beheld his glory, glory of the One and Only who came from the Father, full of grace and truth." (Jn. 1:14)

I remember the very date I first "logged on" to the grace of God. I had been assigned to preach for the 1968 Treasure of Truth campaign in Christchurch, New Zealand. I spent the next nine months preparing those 12 messages. I had decided to center them around the person of Jesus. In my preparation I was caught by the absolute beauty of Jesus, but I couldn't figure out what there was about him that was so beautiful.

One Saturday night toward the end of the nine-month preparation, I sat bolt-right up in the bed. The answer was clear: the beauty of his life that had so attracted me was his limitless kindness toward people. I sat there in bed that night and basked in the glow of his grace. I laid aside the sermon I had prepared for the next morning and preached on "The Limitless Kindness of Jesus." And from that day forward, I have seen Jesus as *the grace of God with skin on it.* And that it is: "From the fullness of his grace we have all received one blessing after another." (Jn.1:16) He is the 'warm body who stood beside us and did all the hard work.' We just enjoy the benefits.

Chapter 13

"The Progression of the Story"

NONE of the parables up to this point got Jesus into serious trouble with the authorities. They were mostly non-threatening, dealing only with seeds and weeds, yeast and fish, flour and farmers, etc. Even the more accusatory explanations of these stories were general in nature, pointing to no one in particular who might take offense.

But in Section II we are confronted with parables which led inexorably to Jesus' death. As the drama intensified, we noticed the shift from "things" to "opinion groups" that began to form among the general public—either in support of or in opposition to Jesus. Now, in the final stage of his ministry, he further narrowed his focus to those men responsible for his execution. He directed his accusations to a single set of opponents: the hypocritical religious leadership, i.e. the Scribes and Pharisees.

In Mt.23:1-38 Jesus reduced the parables to short, incisive indictments hurled in rapid succession at the leaders of the people. He drew graphic word pictures of them "shutting the kingdom of heaven in men's faces; men who would not enter the kingdom nor allow those to enter who were trying to." They would "travel over land and sea to make a single convert and, having done so, they made [the convert] a two-fold more son of hell than themselves," "tithing mint, dill and cumin but neglecting the more important matters of the law—justice, mercy and faith," "blind guides who strain out gnats and swallow camels," hypocritical leaders who were like "whitewashed tombs which look beautiful on the outside but on the inside are full of dead men's bones and everything unclean, full of hypocrisy and wickedness." He called them "snakes, brood of vipers, how can you escape being condemned to hell?"

Then he wept! "O Jerusalem, Jerusalem, you who kill the prophets and stone those sent to you, how often I have longed to gather your children together as a hen gathers her chicks under her wings, but you were not willing. Look, your house is left to you desolate." (Mt.23:37, 38)

We can trace that tragic trajectory through the parables which he used with premeditation, calculation and intention to expose their blindness and to incite the opposition which resulted in his death.

Hugh Schonfield (an avowed critic of Jesus) astutely observed:

> Jesus, knowing full well what he was doing, had quite deliberately forced [the council] …by his skillfully planned and calculated activities…He had himself made doubly sure that they would proceed to extremes against him by goading them with his words and behavior, so that any possible mitigation of their severity would be offset by the personal animus he had intentionally created.[15]

Section II records the obstinate rejection of Jesus by the leaders of the Jewish nation. The ripple effect of that rejection on the common people—both then and now—is the saddest of all stories. We turn now to those stories. "He who has ears had better listen."

---

[15] Hugh J. Schonfield, *The Passover Plot* (New York: Bernard Geis Associates, 1965), p.137.

SECTION II

Chapter 14

"Grace Came Running"

THEY all were gathered around him, eating and enjoying fellowship—those outcasts of society—tax collectors and sinners, the unchurched. And Jesus was right in the middle, unashamedly associating with the best and worst of them. And this wasn't just a one-time thing; it was his custom, so much so it earned him the reputation of being a "glutton and a drunkard, a friend of tax collectors and sinners." (Mt.11: 19)

There was another group standing near, watching and carping: "This man welcomes sinners and eats with them." (Lk.15:1, 2) So, Jesus told them a parable (15:3). Actually he told three parables as he addressed those carpers and their criticism. Three words are common to all three parables: "Lost," "Found," and "Rejoicing." The first parable features a *lost* sheep for which the shepherd, leaving the ninety nine, searched until he *found* it, and there was much *rejoicing*. The second parable pictures a *lost* coin for which the owner searched high and low until she *found* it. She then called her neighbors and friends and said, "*Rejoice* with me; I've *found* my lost coin."

The third parable of this trilogy in Luke 15, however, adds another word to the story: In addition to "lost," "found," and "rejoicing," the word "angry" appears. It's the word Jesus used to describe the attitude of the older brother when he learned that his father was celebrating the return of his wayward brother. The group of critics may not have got the message. They may not have recognized that *they* were the older brother in Jesus' story.

But I wonder if any of us easily recognizes ourself in Jesus' stories? Take an inventory of your life as you consider this parable. Where along this story line do you find yourself? You see, "*This is your life!*" The purpose of this chapter is to cause you, the reader (and me, the author) to examine our life before God.

Act 1 describes five "stations" along the younger son's journey: 1) At home, 2) The Distant Country, 3) Famine and The Pig Pen, 4) Coming to Himself, and 5) Going Home. Act 2 focuses on the older son who remained at home and his attitude toward his father.

These two scenes describe the universal story of the human race. Both deserve our closest attention. ***This is your life!***

ACT I

There was a man who had two sons. The younger one said to his father, 'Father, give me my share of the estate.' So he divided his property between them.

Not long after that, the younger son got together all he had, set off for a distant country and there squandered his wealth in wild living. After he had spent everything, there was a severe famine in that whole country, and he began to be in need. So he went and hired himself out to a citizen of that country, who sent him to his fields to feed pigs. He longed to fill his stomach with the pods that the pigs were eating, but no one gave him anything. When he came to his senses, he said, 'How many of my father's hired servants have food to spare, and here I am starving to death! I will set out and go back to my father and say to him: Father, I have sinned against heaven and against you. I am no longer worthy to be called your son; make me like one of your hired servants.' So he got up and went to his father.

But while he was still a long way off, his father saw him and was filled with compassion for him; he ran to his son, threw his arms around him and kissed him. The son said to him,

'Father, I have sinned against heaven and against you. I am no longer worthy to be called your son.' But the father said to his servants, 'Quick! Bring the best robe and put it on him. Put a ring on his finger and sandals on his feet. Bring the fattened calf and kill it. Let's have a feast and celebrate, for this son of mine was dead and is alive again; he was lost and is found.' So they began to celebrate. (Lk.15:11-34)

The story opens AT HOME. The first words spoken come from the younger brother: He comes to his father and says: *"Give me my..."* Do you recognize anything familiar in these three words? Jesus wasted no time touching the nerve at the center of mankind's fallen state: *Selfishness.* We are born with it; it is the genetic flaw in our sin-scarred, human DNA. There is nothing more central to man's depravity than selfishness. Jesus doesn't go far into the story before exposing it: "There was a man who had two sons. The younger one said to his father, 'Father, give me my share of the estate.' So he divided his property between them." (Lk.15:11-12)

Just how inappropriate was this request? Henri Nouwen, in his classic work,[16] points out the atrocious nature of the request. He says it was equivalent to wishing his father dead! Nouwen quotes Kenneth Bailey's graphic description of just how serious the offense was.[17]

> *For over fifteen years I have been asking people of all walks of life from Morocco to India and from Turkey to the Sudan about the implications of a son's request for his inheritance while his father was still living. The answer has always been emphatically the same...the conversation runs as follows:*
> *Has anyone ever made such a request in your village?*
> *Never!*
> *Could anyone ever make such a request?*
> *Impossible!*
> *If anyone ever did, what would happen?*

---

[16] Henri Nouwen, *The Return of the Prodigal Son* (New York, Doubleday, 1994), p.35.

[17] Ibid.

His father would beat him, of course!
Why?
The request means he wants his father to die.

Jesus says the father granted the younger son's request. "Not long after that, the younger son got together all he had and set off for a distant country." God has granted each of us the same freedom. And each of us has done exactly what the younger son did: we packed our bags and headed for...

THE DISTANT COUNTRY. *"...he set out for a distant country and there squandered his wealth in wild living"* (15:13). We can imagine how he wasted his substance. It won't take us long to conjure up images in our minds because each of us has our own 'foreign country.' He turned to his own way, lived high on the hog, what he wanted he took—as one political figure once said of his own immoral actions: he did it "Because he could." Some go deeper into the pig pen than others, but go we all do.

Jesus' use of the word *"distant"* country leaves the impression that the younger son wanted to put as much space between him and his father as he could, intentionally turning his back on anything to do with his father and his heritage. He wanted freedom. Who of us has not wanted the same thing? And taken the same route?

The key to understanding this parable is realizing that the "distant country" is not a geographical location. It is in the parable but not in the lesson contained in the parable. The distant country in life is the isolated and alienated heart, caused by selfishness. *You can go to the distant country without ever leaving your house!* Selfishness that alienates you from parents is the distant country. A teen storming into her room, slamming the door and pouting because she didn't get her way is that distant country. Wives and husbands, selfish and unforgiving, are that distant country. Brother against brother, neighbor against neighbor. The distant country is *alienation of the heart*—from family, friends and God.

Some *do* leave home. I remember seeing a picture of such a person some years ago in an Oklahoma newspaper. The photo showed a cheap motel room, the lifeless body of a sixteen year old girl, dirty, pregnant, and sprawled on a filthy bed. She had overdosed. What a wasting of her substance; what a squandering of her wealth! She had within her the potential to be a loving mother, nurturing and caring. But she took the wrong road, and it led her—as it did the young prodigal—to:

FAMINE AND THE PIG PEN. *"After he had spent everything, there was a severe famine in that whole country, and he began to be in need."* Selfishness always brings famine. The emptiness that alienation brings never lets up; the alienated person goes through life estranged and isolated—even in the midst of those one thinks are friends. When the funds evaporate, so do those who hang around for the drinks and thrills. In desperation this young Jewish boy hired out to a stranger in the foreign land, and the stranger sent him into the fields to do a job totally foreign to a Jewish lad—feeding swine! Had someone told him as he walked out the door of his father's house, "It won't be long before you'll be feeding pigs," he would have said, "You're crazy, man, I'll never feed pigs." But he did.

How many young people end up making decisions that lead to famine and a pig pen! Oh, not a literal pig pen. They just end up doing things they never dreamed they would do. The first drink of alcohol at a party seems so cool, but that decision has led many to sell their soul for a drink. A young boy starts smoking to prove he's a man only to end up with lung cancer, shackled to an oxygen canister. Or, deciding to drop out of school because it is too hard work, only to spend the rest of life doing work that really *is* hard. Like the Oklahoma girl, as the song goes, "I know what I was feeling, but *what was I thinking*?! Famine is the result of *wrong thinking*! But famine should make one re-think—hopefully, before it is too late.

HE CAME TO HIS SENSES. What a strange expression! It is also universal—this sudden awakening within when one suddenly realizes where he or she is and knows he or she has taken a wrong turn. The fog lifts, the picture clears, the eyes open and the needle of one's inner compass swings 180 degrees. One's whole world swings around.

"When he came to his senses..." is the finest hour in a sinner's life. One might think the finest hour is when a prodigal arrives back home—and that is indeed the desired end result. But the turning point—when poverty of spirit and mourning overwhelm a prodigal—in a sense, trumps even that. Return home he must, but there is no genuine return home without first "coming to one's senses." Fortunately for this young boy, it didn't take much of the pig pen to cause him to make up his mind to:

GO HOME. And this is one thing that is so amazing about the story: What brought the boy to his senses were not noble motives—how he had embarrassed his father and brought shame on the family name, etc. The simple fact that brought him to his senses was this: he was hungry—so hungry he could have eaten the slop he was feeding the pigs. In his mind's eye—and nose—he could see and smell the bread his father's servants were eating. And they had "food to spare, and here I am starving to death." 'Maybe I can go back, not as a son but as a servant. Surely I can go back and work as a servant; I'll ask my father to make me as one of his hired servants.' With this in mind, he got up and began the journey home.

But, wonder of wonders, Jesus paints the picture which lets us see that even motives less than noble are acceptable to God. Surely that can't be true! But surely it *is* true. There is no other option; the prodigal's motives were no less ignoble than ours when we turn back to God. We all come to God out of emptiness, or we don't come. "God has bound all men over to disobedience so that he may have mercy on them all." (Rom.11:32) *Grace has no appeal to those who feel no need.* "Blessed are the poor in spirit" is the first door into the kingdom. Fullness is a brick wall blocking our path to God. It is emptiness that, by the grace of God, opens a door and beckons us home. Fullness makes it terribly difficult, if not impossible, for a rich man to enter the kingdom of God. Only the hungry hurry home!

What thoughts must have haunted him on his journey home: "I've wasted my inheritance! What will my father say? What will he do?" Well, what *would* the father do? (More importantly, how did Jesus picture the action of the father?) He *could* have described the father responding in various ways. The father could have seen the boy coming and turned quickly into the house to wait for the boy to knock on the door and come groveling at his feet. He could have said—much like Potter, the greedy banker in *It's a Wonderful Life,* said to bankrupt George Bailey: "Well, well, well," So you've run out of money, and you've come here expecting me to finance you!" And Potter sent Bailey away empty!

But that's not the picture Jesus painted of the father. Instead, "While [the prodigal] was still a long way off, his father saw him and was filled with compassion for him; he ran to his son, threw his arms around him and kissed him!" And he didn't even let the boy finish his prepared speech. The boy got no further than "I'm not worthy to be called your son."

But the father said to his servants, "Quick! Bring the best robe and put it on him. Let's have a feast and celebrate. This son of mine was dead and is alive again; he was lost and is found. So they began to celebrate." (Lk.15:22-24)

What a picture Jesus painted of the father: full of grace! Grace came running! Grace came hugging, Grace came kissing, Grace came forgiving and Grace came celebrating!! Marvel of marvels!! This is why Jesus was eating with tax collectors and sinners. The carping crowd of critics had their answer—whether they recognized it or not. I wonder if they made the connection. Did they, per chance, connect the dots? *Jesus eating with sinners was a demonstration of the father running to meet the prodigal.*

Where in this drama do you find yourself? Grace will come running. You don't have to prepare a speech. Just come home. "Amazing grace, how sweet the sound that saved a wretch like me; I once was lost, but now I'm found; was blind, but now I see."

You say you didn't recognize yourself at any of the five stations mentioned? Then you may be the older brother. He's just now coming in from the field. Let's pay attention as the curtain rises on Act II of this drama.

Chapter 15

"Grace Came Pleading"

ACT II — The Older Brother

(He had just finished a long day's work and was coming in from the field.)

> MEANWHILE, the older son was in the field. When he came near the house, he heard music and dancing. So he called one of the servants and asked him what was going on. 'Your brother has come,' he replied, 'and your father has killed the fattened calf because he has him back safe and sound.' The older brother became angry and refused to go in. So his father went out and pleaded with him. But he answered his father, 'Look! All these years I've been slaving for you and never disobeyed your orders. Yet you never gave me even a young goat so I could celebrate with my friends. But when this son of yours who has squandered your property with prostitutes comes home, you kill the fattened calf for him!' 'My son,' the father said, 'you are always with me, and everything I have is yours. But we had to celebrate and be glad, because this brother of yours was dead and is alive again; he was lost and is found.' (15:25-32)

It is just here that the fourth word, "angry," appears: "*The older brother became angry and refused to go in.*" One might wish Act II had not been included in this drama. It throws a wet blanket on an occasion of celebration. But Jesus, as always, revealed reality; this is just the way life is. There will always be those who can't bear the thought of others being blessed –others who don't deserve it—who haven't earned the right to be so blessed, and certainly to be blessed over and above themselves. That's just not fair!

The first time the word "angry" appears in the Bible is in Gen.4:5—*"So Cain was very angry, and his face was downcast."* Though a somewhat different situation, the result is the same, and the characters are the same. In both cases, the older brother is the angry one; angry over his younger brother being given something he thinks belongs to him. Anger led Cain to kill his brother and anger led the older son in Jesus' story to do virtually the same.

Listen as Jesus pictures the older brother venting his anger:

"Look, all these years I have been slaving for you and never disobeyed your orders." You'll have to hand it to this older brother: he had not gone off and wasted his inheritance in some far off land. He had stayed home and worked. And the father didn't deny that. In fact he said, *"My son, you are always with me, and everything I have is yours."* (In that culture the first born received a double portion.) But that wasn't good enough for the older son. It didn't satisfy him that the grace of his father covered him; he didn't want his father's grace to extend beyond him!

His accusation revealed two attitudes toward his father. Jesus used two expressions to paint in dark colors the older son's reaction: *"slaving for you"* and *"you never gave me even a young goat so I could celebrate with my friends."* With the words "all these years I have been *slaving* for you" Jesus described the older son's estrangement and alienation from his father—even though the son remained at home. The older son didn't say, "All these years I have loved you," or "All these years I've worked side by side with you." But "all these years I have been *slaving* for you." His words reveal a distant and cold relationship with the father. He had, indeed, been in geographical proximity with his father, but he is not pictured as having been in a loving relationship with him. What was true of the younger brother was true also of the older: *You don't have to leave home to be estranged.*

His words also show resentful ingratitude: *"You never gave me even a goat to celebrate with my friends."* Jesus must have intentionally crafted this story to call special attention to the ingratitude of the group of critics. He could have had the son saying, "You never gave me a fattened calf…" which in itself would have revealed ingratitude. But he has the son saying, "You never gave me even a *goat*." If gratitude is the highest response one can give God's grace, resentful ingratitude is the lowest and most offensive.

His defense also reveals an implacable resistance to reconciliation with his brother. His words to his father describing his brother as "this son of yours" show just how far he had gone in his alienation. His father's pleading for "this brother of yours" had no effect on the older brother. Reconciliation was out of the picture. He wanted no connection with the young brother, and thus he cut himself off from both his father and his brother.

The story also reveals entrenched rebellion as it describes *where* the confrontation took place. The older son is not pictured as going into the house to find his father and accuse him. No, it's just the opposite; the older brother "*refused to go in.*" It was his father who "went out and pleaded with him" (15:28). Here again we see Jesus picture the father as taking the initiative: he "went out and pleaded." Grace came running to the younger son; Grace came pleading with the older son. In both cases the father is shown pursuing his sons. If there is any one picture of God revealed in the Scriptures, it is of a God who pursues; a God who initiates.

C. S. Lewis' description of his own conversion (briefly alluded to above and reminiscent of Frances Thompson's poem, "Hound of Heaven"), tells how he finally gave in to this One who so persistently pursued him:

> You must picture me alone in that room in Magdalen, night after night, feeling, whenever my mind lifted even for a second from my work, the steady unrelenting approach of Him whom I desired so earnestly not to meet. That which I greatly feared had at last come upon me. In the Trinity term of 1929 I gave in, and admitted that God was God, and knelt and prayed: perhaps, that night, the most dejected and reluctant convert in all England. I did not then see what is now the most shining and obvious thing: the Divine humility which will accept a convert even on such terms. The prodigal son at least walked home on his own feet. But who can duly admire that Love which will open the high gates to a prodigal who is

brought in kicking, struggling, resentful, and darting his eyes in every direction for a chance to escape.[18]

In all of Jesus' depictions of his Father, he consistently pictures him as the God who pursues: In the parables God is always the initiator. It is God who "plants a vineyard," "prepares a feast," "sends his son," "hires workers," "forgives debts," "forgives sins," "prepares a wedding" "searches for a lost sheep," he runs, he pleads. God is always on the move. "My father is always at his work to this very day, and I, too, am working." (Jn.5:17)

And the Jewish nation? How is it pictured—not just in Jesus' parables but throughout their own Scriptures? It is pictured as an unfaithful wife, a son who promises to go to work but doesn't; or, as in this parable, the older brother who refuses to respond to God's pleading. The martyr Stephen summed it up succinctly: "You stiff-necked people! Your hearts and ears are still uncircumcised. You are just like your ancestors: You always resist the Holy Spirit!" (Acts 7:50-52). Grace came pleading but, for the most part, the Jewish nation (especially the leaders) would have no part of it: "He came to his own, but his own didn't receive him." (Jn.1:11)

The continuing disregard of God by that favored nation and the ultimate consequences it suffered should be a wake-up call to America. We are, at this present time, pursuing the same path of rebellion ancient Israel pursued. Unless America heeds God's call to return to him, we can expect no different consequence than what they suffered. We are presently experiencing a moral decline unprecedented in our history, and that decline is increasing exponentially with every passing day. The financial melt down is not the problem; it's only one of the consequences of turning away from God. As with ancient Israel, unless America returns to God, it will be said of these United States:

> The LORD, the God of their ancestors, sent word to them through his messengers again and again, because he had pity on his people and on his dwelling place. But they mocked God's messengers, despised his words and scoffed at his prophets until the wrath of the LORD was aroused against his people and there was no remedy. (2Chron.36:15, 16)

---

[18] C. S. Lewis, *Surprised By Joy* (London Geofrey Bles, 1955) pp.214,15.

Chapter 16

"'In Your Face' Grace"

I T ALL BEGAN with a conversation between Jesus and Peter as they watched a 'rich young man' turn away from Jesus with downcast face upon hearing the condition, "If you want to be perfect, go sell your possessions and give to the poor, and you will have treasure in heaven. Then, come, follow me." (Matt.19:21)

It was the next statement that startled Peter and the rest of the Twelve:

> I tell you the truth, it is hard for a rich man to enter the kingdom of heaven. Again I tell you, it is easier for a camel to go through the eye of a needle than for a rich man to enter into the kingdom of God. (Mt.19:23-24)
>
> When the disciples heard this, they were greatly astonished and asked, 'Who then can be saved?' (v. 25) Jesus looked at them and said, 'With man this is impossible, but with God all things are possible.' (v.26)

Then Peter injected his personal opinion of the investment the Twelve had made in Jesus' cause. Said Peter, "We have left everything to follow you; what then will there be for us?" This requires no translation: "What's in it for *me*?" is the universal equivalent to Peter's question. But Jesus acknowledged that there is reward for such sacrifice. Jesus said to them:

> I tell you the truth, at the renewal of all things, when the Son of Man sits on his glorious throne, you who have followed me will

133

sit on twelve thrones, judging the twelve tribes of Israel. And everyone who has left houses or brothers or sisters or father or mother or children or fields for my sake will receive a hundred times as much and will inherit eternal life. (Mt.19:27-29)

But then came the shocker: *"But, many who are first will be last, and many who are last will be first."* (19:30) Jesus had done it again: he turned everything upside-down. And, to illustrate his point, he told a very startling parable (Mt.20:1-15). Then, to emphasize his point, he repeated the shocker in an even more restrictive form at the conclusion of the parable (20:16)— *"So the last will be first and the first will be last."* These two bolts of lightning serve as bookends to the parable contained between them. The parable in between runs so counter to what we consider right that we want to cry out, *"That's not fair!"* But, before we explode, hear the Lord say, "This is what the kingdom of heaven is like." (20:1) End of argument!

> For the kingdom of heaven is like a landowner who went out early in the morning to hire workers for his vineyard. He agreed to pay them a denarius for the day and sent them into his vineyard. About nine in the morning he went out and saw others standing in the marketplace doing nothing. He told them, "You also go and work in my vineyard, and I will pay you whatever is right." So they went. He went out again about noon and about three in the afternoon and did the same thing. About five in the afternoon he went out and found still others standing around. He asked them, "Why have you been standing here all day long doing nothing?" "Because no one has hired us," they answered. He said to them, "You also go and work in my vineyard."
>
> When evening came, the owner of the vineyard said to his foreman, "Call the workers and pay them their wages, beginning with the last ones hired and going on to the first."
>
> The workers who were hired about five in the afternoon came and each received a denarius. So when those came who were hired first, they expected to receive more. But each one of them also received a denarius. When they received it, they began to grumble against the landowner. "These who were hired last worked only one hour," they said, "and you have made them equal to us who have borne the burden of the

work and the heat of the day." But he answered one of them, "I am not being unfair to you, friend. Didn't you agree to work for a denarius? Take your pay and go. I want to give the one who was hired last the same as I gave you. Don't I have the right to do what I want with my own money? Or are you envious because I am generous?"

So the last will be first, and the first will be last. (Matt.20:1-15)

Why would Jesus paint such a picture of the kingdom? Could not he have been a bit more gentle? Could not he have had the owner of the vineyard instruct the foreman to pay the all-day workers first and send them home and then pay the same wage to the eleventh-hour men after the all-day workers were out of sight? Would not that also have been "grace?" Yes, it would have been. The eleventh-hour workers would have been shown grace, for they hadn't done the work the all-day workers had done, yet they had received the same pay. Then, why did he construct the story the way he did? Why did he "rub the noses" of the Twelve in it? He patterned this parable intentionally in order to make it plain that the reward for working in his vineyard is not a matter of merit but of grace. God's grace will be extended to those we consider undeserving, whether we like it or not.

And that in itself is an oxymoron. For, the very definition of grace is "favor shown to those who don't deserve it." So, "Where's the beef?" It's at the same location it was in the older son's complaint. "That's not fair!" he cried to his father when he didn't receive what he thought he had earned—what "he had slaved for all those years." The root of all such complaints is pride and selfishness. And Jesus had to do this root canal on the Twelve and on all his followers in every age to extract this abscess from our egos.

For the sake of argument, let's say that we are the eleventh-hour workers; we've come on the scene only in the last 200 years. Some others have made their contributions hundreds of years before we came along. (There will always be those who have been in the vineyard longer, worked harder, given more liberally, loved more dearly, believed more strongly, suffered more intensely, etc.) At the end of life's day when we all stand before God to receive our reward, could it be that those early workers will be required to stand aside and allow us "Johnny-Come-Latelies" to go first and receive our "pay?"

But again, for the sake of argument, let us assume that we are the all-day workers. We (so we think) have discerned more accurately, have believed more strongly, loved …, worked…, given … etc, etc, more than others. At the end of life's day when we go before God's throne to receive our "pay," we will have to stand aside and let people we think unworthy go ahead of us and receive the same pay! (There will always be those we think don't have quite as much on the ball as we, whom we perceive to be not as doctrinally sound or pure as we, or who used a different pick or shovel in doing their work, or who came along years after we had entered the vineyard.) Will we have to stand aside and let them go first and receive the pay we feel we deserve? That's what the parable seems to imply. (Don't get nervous; God knows who is in his vineyard and who isn't. He knows whom he hired. He won't pay anyone who is not in his vineyard/kingdom.)

But if you *are* nervous or upset, before you write me off completely, go with me to a hill on the northwest side of Jerusalem and watch a scene that may change your mind. It's the sight of an execution. There are three crosses erected: two thieves occupy the crosses on either side of another cross—that of a Jewish rabbi—Jesus, the man who told the "Vineyard" parable. Let's go up close so we can hear what's being said. Jesus' long-time followers and friends are there—watching and waiting. We draw close enough to hear a brief exchange between Jesus and one of the thieves who, by his own admission, deserved his punishment. This faceless, nameless, hopeless thief makes a bold plea: "Jesus, remember me when you come into your kingdom." (Lk.23:42)

Amazed as we may be at the audacity of the thief in making this request, it is Jesus' response that causes us to stand in awe with our hand over our mouth in wonder and amazement. Jesus answered, "Today, you will be with me in Paradise." (Lk.23:44) There it was! He made his three-year workers stand aside and watch him usher into Paradise a one-hour, undeserving sinner who begged for mercy.

Do you realize what we just saw? We just saw Jesus, in his dying hour, present himself as the owner of the vineyard who could "do what he wanted with his own money." And the question he asked in his parable should haunt us, "Are you envious because I am generous?"

Jesus introduced the parable (Mt.20:1) with these words, "For the kingdom of heaven is like [this]." If our Lord, the owner of the vineyard, says that this is what the kingdom of heaven is like, I think we'll be wise not to try to change it, don't you? "But..." But nothing! "Take your pay and go; I want to give the man who was hired last the same as I gave you."

Chapter 17

"Grace With a Hook"

"EVER SINCE this church learned about grace, there's never been enough food at our church suppers!" I laughed when I first heard that simple complaint. Evidently several members of that church had heard the message of grace and had relaxed their culinary contributions. But had they heard the message of grace accurately? Or had they misunderstood? If they had, they weren't the first or only ones to misunderstand grace. Some Christians in Rome and Galatia and other places also had misunderstood—and in more serious ways than just a few apple pies missing from the dessert table.

In fact, the subject of grace was probably the most misunderstood subject of all among the first century Christians. Some wanted to add circumcision to grace, thus creating a legalism—turning freedom in Christ back into bondage (Acts 15:1; Gal.5:1-6). Others wanted to eliminate holiness from grace, thus creating a libertinism—turning liberty into license (Gal.5:13, 16-21). 'How quickly the Galatians had deserted him who had called them by the grace of Christ and had turned to another gospel!' (Gal.1:6)

Well, what is the true nature of grace? Our son Jon often makes insightful theological observations. Here's one that took me off guard. He said, "Dad, God's love is unconditional but not his grace." I was a bit slow to see his point, but it eventually became clear. I knew God's love was unconditional;

God doesn't love us because we deserve it (conditionally) but in spite of (unconditionally). "You see, at just the right time, Christ died for the ungodly ... God commends his love for us in that while we were yet sinners, Christ died for us." (Rom.5:6, 8) So, "God's love is unconditional...

...but not his grace." Thus, the title of this chapter: "Grace With a Hook." There are certain obligations connected to grace. But, someone may object, "How can grace be grace if there are conditions attached to it?" Does God change his mind and take back his gift of forgiveness? Jesus answers in his usual manner: with a parable. Listen up:

This parable, like the previous one, was rooted in a conversation between Jesus and Peter. Peter asked Jesus, "Lord, how many times shall I forgive my brother when he sins against me? Up to seven times?" It appears Peter was offering to go beyond the customary limit of four which Jewish tradition had come to allow. But, here again, Jesus went beyond the expected. Jesus replied, "I tell you, not seven times, but seventy seven times." (Mt.18:22)

> Therefore, the kingdom of heaven is like a king who wanted to settle accounts with his servants. As he began the settlement, a man who owed him ten thousand talents was brought to him. Since he was not able to pay, his master ordered that he and his wife and his children and all that he had be sold to repay the debt. The servant fell on his knees before him. 'Be patient with me' he begged, 'and I will pay back everything.' The servant's master took pity on him, cancelled the debt and let him go.

> But when that servant went out, he found one of his fellow servants who owed him a hundred denarii. He grabbed him and began to choke him. 'Pay back what you owe me,' he said. His fellow servant fell to his knees and begged him, 'Be patient with me,' he said, 'and I will pay you back.' But he refused. Instead he went off and had the man thrown into prison until he could pay back the debt.

> When the other servants saw what had happened, they were greatly distressed and went and told their master everything that had happened. Then the master called the servant in. 'You wicked servant,' he said, 'I cancelled all that debt of yours because you begged me to. Shouldn't you have had mercy on your fellow servant just as I had on you?' In anger

his master turned him over to the jailers to be tortured until he should pay back all he owed. (Matt.18:23-34)

To make sure his disciples understood the lesson, he added: "This is how my heavenly Father will treat each one of you unless you forgive your brother from your heart." (Mt.20:35)

To make sure *we* understand the lesson, let's identify the characters in this story. Let's start first with an easy one: Who is the king in the story? Well, that's easy enough; the king is God. (Jesus always relinquished the highest position to his Father.) Secondly: Who is the servant who owed the King ten thousand talents? That was Peter; and it is you and I. (Don't stop now to list all the things you owe God.) Thirdly: Who is the fellow servant who owed the 100 denarii (about $20)? He was Peter's (and our) fellow servant who offended Peter or you or me. You know, the brother who made some less-than-kind remark, or the sister who just looked a certain way that you *interpreted* as demeaning or rude. (All the while the offender may have just had a crick in his neck! I know of such a case.) And we're not going to forgive *that rude remark*??? We're going to put him or her in an emotional jail to which we alone have the key and hold the poor soul there until the last penny of penance and apology is paid?

You are on your way to church. You're late, you can't find a parking space except down in the lower 40, so you're already out of sorts, as well as out of breath from the long walk. You go inside the auditorium late and sit down just as they are serving the Lord's Supper. And, you look over and see that brother who made you mad because … Oh, you can't remember what it was.

Of course there are more serious offenses people suffer, and I'm not making light of them: physical abuse suffered by battered wives, sexual abuse suffered by children whose innocence has been ripped from them, emotional abuse from words spoken in anger or out of hate—abuse never repented of; damage that can't be undone and the memory of which may lurk and linger for years. Forgiving may be less difficult than forgetting, but the failing of the latter need not imply the absence of the former. Some memory scars may remain after the forgiveness has been complete.

But, here comes the loaf—the one loaf of which both you and your offender are members (ICor.10:16, 17). What are you going to do? Well, you know what Jesus said for you to do: "Leave your gift at the altar and go, be reconciled to your brother, and then come and offer your gift" (Matt.5:24). I wonder what would happen if we actually did what Jesus commanded. If, before the Supper is served some Sunday morning, a shepherd of the flock stands up and calls for a time of confession and reconciliation, saying: "If anyone has anything against another, now is the time to set things right—before we eat the Supper." Only good would come, healing would take place, release and joy would flow.

I, as the preacher, tried that once; nobody moved—they were shocked and too embarrassed to take the first step toward reconciliation—certainly not in public! But afterwards, in the foyer two women were in each other's arms weeping. One said to the other, "I owe you an apology; fifteen years ago you offended me, and I never told you; I just kept it in. Please forgive me." And they both wept.

I personally know it works. Once I offended one of my sons. I knew it; he knew it. It had happened earlier in the week. Now it was time to go to church, time to eat the bread, drink the cup of the One we both had offended many times. I couldn't stand to just sit! I leaned over to him and said, "Let's go into my office; I need to say something to you." We went; stood face to face. I said, "I know I offended you last week. Now we're about to eat the Supper of the Lord. Before we eat, I'm asking you to forgive me." He and I embraced and wept, then went in and sat together—really *together!* That action forged a bond between us that nothing can break. It was sealed by the blood of the one who had died for us both.

Grace is not a broom designed for sweeping things under the rug; it is a gift from God intended to change us. Who has not wept while watching Jean Val Jean in *Les Miserables*? Having stolen some silver items from the monastery, he was caught red handed by the police and brought back to the priest for identification and to be sent back to prison. I could not restrain the tears when the priest said, "Why did you not take the candlestick also? I gave them both to you." That one gesture (quite a stretch of the facts, to say the least) saved Jean Val Jean's life and changed him forever. He spent the rest of his life serving and forgiving others.

Something similar happened to me recently. I was making plans to excavate under our house, preparing for the exterminator to treat the house for termites. Before I began excavating I met a man who was unemployed. I didn't relish crawling under the house by myself, and he was out of work, so I asked him if he wanted a job. He accepted. We crawled under the house, and I showed him what was needed, gave him the tools and, by agreement, everything was set. I had to leave town, so I left him in charge. I left $500 with the church office to pay him each day for his work. Each day he was to go by the church office, report his hours and collect his pay. This he did faithfully. He also called me each day and told me exactly what he had done—how far he had dug, etc.

When I returned, I went under the house and found—guess what? Not one single shovel full of dirt had been removed!! Not one! He had robbed me of $500. The man was an ex-convict, so he was in serious trouble. Some weeks later I saw him walking down the street. And he saw me see him, and he started walking fast. I wheeled around thinking, "I've got you now." He turned into a dead end street, and I followed him. I had him cornered; all I had to do was call 911, have him arrested, and he would be in jail again.

But, I also was cornered—by my Lord. I had to make a decision: Having been forgiven of all my sins (which were numerous, to say the least), I was now being put on trial before the Lord. Would I call 911 and have this man thrown back in jail? Or would I forgive him and let him go free? This parable had "cornered" me, and I had to decide. I rolled down the window and said, "You didn't do me right, you know." He said, "Yes, sir, I didn't. I'm sorry." I had no choice but to forgive him! Well, I did have a choice, but I didn't like the consequences of the other option!

Jesus said the forgiveness must come "from the heart" (Mt.18:35). I found that, having made the decision to forgive him, I was released as well as he— he from theft and deception, I from resentment and anger. He and I have since become friends; who knows where this story will end. Whatever the outcome, he and I both have experienced "grace with a hook" and, hopefully, have emerged better men. Parables have a way of nailing you!!

Paul remarked to the Romans, "Do you not realize that God's kindness (grace) is intended to lead you to repentance"(paraphrase of Rom.2:4). Paul urged the believers in Corinth "not to accept God's grace in vain" (II Cor.6:1). God's grace is not unconditional. It must be passed on, or it will be retracted. When the servant refused to forgive his fellow servant, his

Lord called him in and took back the grace that had been given him. And Jesus concluded: "This is how your heavenly Father will treat each of you unless you forgive your brother *from your heart.*" (emphasis mine)

So, grace is wonderful, but it's not unconditional; we either pass it on or we lose it. That's the "hook" in grace.

Chapter 18

Grace Rejected

JUST as there are responsibilities that go with accepting grace, there are also consequences which follow rejecting grace. One of the major themes of Jesus' "grace stories" is the theme "Grace Rejected." More space in the Gospels is devoted to this theme than to any other parable theme. And these parables dealing with rejection escalate (both in number and in severity) toward the end of Jesus' ministry. The last week of his life is full of them, especially the Tuesday before his execution.

But the Jews' rejection of God began long before Jesus was even born. It can be said with little fear of contradiction that the Jewish nation didn't want God. They wanted him when they were in trouble, but once out of trouble they returned to the gods of their neighbors. All of the prophets bear witness to this. Surprisingly, in the same chapter in which it was prophesied "I will open my mouth in parables, I will reveal hidden things, things from of old" (Ps.78), there follows a long list of accusations against the Jewish people. After recounting the many blessings God had poured out on them (78:3-31) the psalmist says, "In spite of all this, they kept on sinning; in spite of his wonders, they did not believe. So he ended their days in futility and their years in terror." (v.33)

The psalmist continues his accusations throughout the 78th psalm, too numerous to list here (at least 15 separate allegations against the children of Israel) charging them with constant rebellion: He sums it up by saying:

"How often they rebelled against him in the desert and grieved him in the wasteland. Again and again they put God to the test; they vexed the Holy One of Israel." (vv.40, 41)

As thoroughly as the 78th Psalm lays out the case against the Jewish nation, it is only a token of the entirety of the Hebrew prophets' charges of rebellion by the Jewish nation. Ezekiel chapter 16 is a graphic narrative of the history of the nation, starting as a new-born babe wallowing in its own birth fluids—cord not cut, etc. But the baby grew up and became beautiful and eligible for marriage. God saw her and took her as his bride, loved her and lavished her with gifts and fine clothing. But sadly, she rejected her husband and turned to prostitution. She left her husband (Jehovah) and actually paid foreign lovers to ravish her. The sad conclusion to this rebellion is recorded throughout the chronicles of their national history.

Jesus knew his nation's history, and he summed it up succinctly: "I know you. I know that you do not have the love of God in your hearts." (Jn.5:42) That was the bottom line. John's assessment sixty years later was "He came to that which was his own, but his own did not receive him." (Jn.1:11) Nothing is clearer in the history of the Jewish nation than the fact that basically the Jew did not want Jehovah, nor did they want what Jesus had to offer in the name of Jehovah. Continuing the prophets' warnings, Jesus told the rejection parables.

Two of these "rejection" parables had national implications and, as such, had historical significance and were thus prophetic in nature. One of them, spoken somewhat earlier by Jesus (Lk.14:16-24), serves as an introduction to the later, more severe indictment of the Jewish leaders. In this parable Jesus told of a man who prepared a great banquet and invited many guests. When the banquet was ready the man sent his servant to tell those who had been invited, "Come, for everything is now ready." In this story, the invited ones, though dismissive, were ostensibly polite. Jesus replied:

> A certain man was preparing a great banquet and invited many guests. At the time of the banquet he sent his servant to tell those who had been invited, 'Come, for everything is now ready.' But they all alike began to make excuses. The first said, 'I have just bought a field, and I must go and see it. Please excuse me.'

Another said, 'I have just bought five yoke of oxen, and I'm on my way to try them out. Please excuse me.' Still another said, 'I just got married, so I can't come.'

The servant came back and reported this to his master. Then the owner of the house became angry and ordered his servant, 'Go out quickly into the streets and alleys of the town and bring in the poor, the crippled, the blind and the lame.'

'Sir,' the servant said, 'what you ordered has been done, but there is still room.' Then the master told his servant, 'Go out to the roads and country lanes and compel them to come in, so that my house will be full. I tell you, not one of those who were invited will get a taste of my banquet.'

The historical implications of this parable agree with the same story line in the later, more severe stories. The ones first invited represented the Jews. This theme runs through not only the other rejection parables but also through the later history of the spread of the gospel as recorded in Acts of the Apostles. It is acknowledged also in the writings of Paul. It always had been God's plan to offer the invitation to the Jews first. Jesus' instructions before his ascension held to this plan: "You will be my witnesses in Jerusalem, and in all Judea and Samaria, and to the ends of the earth." (Acts 1:8) Paul always went to the Jews first and then to the Gentiles. Later he wrote that the gospel was the "power of God for the salvation of everyone who believes: first for the Jew, then for the Gentile." (Rom.1:16) So it doesn't require any special insight to understand that the ones who were first invited represented the Jewish nation.

The rejection of Jesus began innocently enough: they were amazed at him when he was twelve years of age (Lk.2:47); they were further amazed at him when he was thirty "because he taught as one who had authority." (Mt.7:29) At first they spoke favorably of him in Nazareth…and "were amazed at the gracious words that came from his lips." (Lk 4:22) But by the end of that Sabbath-day service they were so furious with him they tried to kill him. This event in Nazareth turned out to be a microcosm of his entire ministry.

The most severe of these rejection parables is found in Mt.21:33-42, spoken on the Tuesday before his death. It served as the final exhibit in Jesus' evidence against his people:

Listen to another parable: There was a landowner who planted a vineyard. He put a wall around it, dug a winepress in it and built a watchtower. Then he rented the vineyard to some farmers and moved to another place. When the harvest time approached, he sent his servants to the tenants to collect his fruit. "The tenants seized his servants; they beat one, killed another, and stoned a third. Then he sent other servants to them, more than the first time, and the tenants treated them the same way.

It is here that Jesus injects himself into the parable:

Last of all, he sent his son to them. 'They will respect my son,' he said. But when the tenants saw the son, they said to each other, 'This is the heir. Come, let's kill him and take his inheritance.' So they took him and threw him out of the vineyard and killed him. "Therefore, when the owner of the vineyard comes, what will he do to those tenants?" "He will bring those wretches to a wretched end," they replied, "and he will rent the vineyard to other tenants, who will give him his share of the crop at harvest time." Jesus said to them, "Have you never read in the Scriptures:

The stone the builders rejected
has become the cornerstone;
the Lord has done this,
and it is marvelous in our eyes?" (Ps.118:22, 23)

Then Jesus made the application: "Therefore I tell you, that the kingdom of God will be taken away from you and given to a people that will produce its fruit. He who falls on this stone will be broken to pieces, but he on whom it falls will be crushed." (vv.43, 44) But they thumbed their nose and rushed headlong into a national disaster unequaled in human history (Mt.24:21).

Josephus concurred as he recorded the Roman assault against Jerusalem in A.D. 70: "… the war which the Jews made with the Romans hath been the greatest of all those, not only that have been in our times, but, in a manner, of those that were ever heard of."[19]

Jesus predicted in detail the destruction of Jerusalem, and the very thought of it brought him to tears.

> As he approached Jerusalem and saw the city, he wept over it and said, "If you, even you, had only known on this day what would bring you peace—but now it is hidden from your eyes. The days will come upon you when your enemies will build an embankment against you and encircle you and hem you in on every side. They will dash you to the ground, you and the children within your walls. They will not leave one stone on another, because you did not recognize the time of God's coming to you." (Lk.19:41-44)

The Siege of Jerusalem in the year 70 A.D. was a decisive event in the first Jewish-Roman War. The siege was begun in 66 A.D. by General Vespasian and was followed by four years of military assault, disease and starvation producing conditions that defy description. The siege was completed in March of A.D. 70 by General Titus when Vespasian was called to Rome to serve as Emperor after the death of Nero. The Roman army broke through the wall surrounding Jerusalem, slaughtering thousands, and thousands more being taken to Rome as slaves. Estimates of the number of victims vary but generally total over one million.

> The Temple Mount, everywhere enveloped in flames, seemed to be boiling over from its base; yet the blood seemed more abundant than the flames and the numbers of the slain greater than those of the slayers. The soldiers climbed over heaps of bodies as they chased the fugitives.[20]

But that didn't end the rebellion of the Jews or the consequences of their rejection of the grace of God. A remnant of Jewish rebels escaped Jerusa-

---

[19] Flavius Josephus, *The Wars of the Jews*, Book XX, chap. V*III, Preface, Section 1.*

[20] Siege of Jerusalem, Wikipedia.

lem and proceeded to capture and occupy Herod's fortress at Masada. The Roman army, using Jewish prisoners, set to work hauling thousands of tons of earth and stone to construct a ramp 375 feet high abutting the western approach to Masada. In 73 A.D. the Romans stormed the fortress, prepared to kill or capture the rebels by force only to find to their astonishment the bodies of 960 men, women and children—the result of a communal suicide pact. The consequences of rejecting the grace of God are severe and far-reaching—at times, as seen at Masada, even self-inflicted.

Surely, that would be the end of their rebellion; but it wasn't. In 135 A.D. a man by the name of Bar Kochba led yet another rebellion against Rome. This rebellion was the final straw for Rome. The resistance was crushed, and the Roman government expelled all Jews from their homeland. In derision Rome named the land "Palestine," adding insult to injury by naming the Jewish homeland after their hated enemy the Philistines. And it is called Palestine to this day.

When Jesus lamented (Mt.23:37), "Oh Jerusalem, Jerusalem, you who kill the prophets and stone those sent to you, how often I have longed to gather your children together, as a hen gathers her chicks under her wings, but you were not willing," he was not referring to the many times they had rejected him during his three-year ministry; he was talking about the fourteen hundred years of their national history during which they had scorned him and turned "each man to his own way." Their rejection of his grace was virtually total.

Jesus' indictment was consistent with the judgment of all the Hebrew prophets, the Pentateuch and the Psalms of Lament. They have been a persecuted race from their days of bondage in Egypt, and the persecution has continued throughout their national history. Jesus himself described the A.D. 70 destruction of Jerusalem by Rome:

> When you see Jerusalem being surrounded by armies, you will know that its desolation is near. Then let those who are in Judea flee to the mountains, let those in the city get out, and let those in the country not enter the city. For this is the time of punishment in fulfillment of all that has been written. How dreadful it will be in those days for pregnant women and nursing mothers! There will be great distress in the land and wrath against this people. They will fall by the sword and

will be taken as prisoners to all the nations. Jerusalem will be trampled on by the Gentiles until the times of the Gentiles are fulfilled. (Lk.21:20-24)

The consequences of rejecting the grace of God are certain and severe: Five centuries earlier, as Jerusalem was being destroyed by the Babylonians and her citizens being carried into captivity, the concluding remarks describing her demise are filled with pathos and resignation:

> The LORD, the God of their ancestors, sent word to them through his messengers again and again, because he had pity on his people and on his dwelling place. But they mocked God's messengers, despised his words and scoffed at his prophets until the wrath of the LORD was aroused against his people and there was no remedy. (2Chronicles 36:15, 16)

The story of the Jewish race is one of wonder and admiration, of sadness and sympathy. The Jewish people presently lead the entire world in Nobel awards for achievements in science, music, literature, finance, entertainment and in virtually every other field of endeavor. But, at the same time, they are the constant victims of anti-Semitism. Hitler murdered six million; Iran has vowed to "wipe them off the face of the earth."

Yet, they remain; and at times in places of high honor: Queen Victoria asked Benjamin Disraeli—England's Prime Minister of Jewish origin—to give her in one word evidence of the existence of God. Disraeli responded with one word, "Jew." The continuing presence of the Jew can certainly be viewed as strong evidence for the existence of Jehovah, the God of the Jew. (The Jewish nation is the only nation in history whose extensive records claim it was created by their God Jehovah; all other nations created their own gods.) How unique a position the nation of Israel occupies! Some believe the final chapter has yet to be written.

But Israel's presence also is almost "anti-evidence"—not that it refutes the existence of God, but that throughout much of Jewish history "God's name [has been] blasphemed among the Gentiles because of [them]." (Isa.52:5) Their persistent yet paradoxical presence is evidence of not only the love of God but also of the consequences of rejecting that love; consequences of rejecting the grace of God.

What specifically was there in Jesus' teachings to which the Jewish nation so vehemently objected? Can their rejection of him be isolated and identified? *Before* his execution Jesus' claims of deity infuriated the Jewish leaders. But those were just claims. *After* his execution there was one undeniable event which galvanized their opposition. It had to do with an unexpected turn of events for which they were not prepared and for which they had no truthful answer. Let us now investigate that unexpected turn.

SECTION III

Chapter 19

The Unexpected

O N THE MORNING of the 18th of Aviv (Nissan), 4029 (Jewish calendar)[21] the city of Jerusalem was in chaos and confusion. There had been an earthquake earlier that morning (Mt.28:2)—considered perhaps by some an aftershock, for there had been a major quake three days earlier (27:51, 52). That one was preceded by an eclipse of the sun from twelve noon till 3:00 p.m. (27:45). At three o'clock Jesus of Nazareth, having been crucified, had expired. Suddenly an earthquake rocked the city. The temple was damaged, its curtain was torn in two from top to bottom. The earth shook, rocks split open and tombs were exposed (27:45-52).

Now, three days later, rumors were rampant in Jerusalem. A grave reportedly had been robbed, the soldiers guarding the tomb were in trouble for neglect of duty (Mt.28:13), and the Sanhedrin had called an emergency meeting to cope with an unexpected turn of events (28:12). People were accusing each other. One follower of the Nazarene had committed suicide (27:5), and other followers were hiding behind closed doors for fear they would be hunted down and executed (Jn.20:19). Their world had suddenly crumbled beneath them. They had thought Jesus was the one who would redeem Israel and set them free from the hated Roman occupation (Lk.24:21).

---

[21] Eugene Faulstich and Michael J. Rood, "What Time Is It?" *1999 Chronology Books* (Two Harbors, MN: New Moon Publishing, 1999), pp. 20, 21.

How had their dreams so completely evaporated? To begin with, Jesus' fate had been sealed several weeks earlier when the Jewish leaders were informed that he had raised Lazarus of Bethany from the dead. Some who actually had witnessed the event went to the Pharisees and told them what Jesus had done (Jn.11:46). At that point the die was cast: Jesus had to be eliminated. The extent of their rejection of Jesus became obvious as the leaders laid out a plan they considered to be the end of their problem:

> Then the chief priests and the Pharisees called a meeting of the Sanhedrin. "What are we accomplishing?" they asked. "Here is this man performing many miraculous signs. If we let him go on like this, everyone will believe in him, and then the Romans will come and take away both our place and our nation." Then, one of them, named Caiaphas, who was high priest that year, spoke up, "You know nothing at all! You do not realize that it is better for you that one man die for the people than that the whole nation perish." (Jn.11:47-50)

As the plot unfolded, the leaders were reminded of Jesus' puzzling claim: "Destroy this temple, and I will raise it again in three days." (Jn.2:19) The leaders decided to use that statement for their initial charge against him. The leaders were willing to accept even conflicting testimony to establish that charge (Mk.14:57-59). But, seemingly frustrated at the pace of the trial and the inconsistency of the testimony, the chief priest resorted to an illegality: he demanded one accused of a capital crime to incriminate himself. "I charge you under oath by the living God: Tell us if you are the Christ, the Son of God!" "Yes, it is as you say," Jesus replied. "But I say to all of you: In the future you will see the Son of Man sitting at the right hand of the Mighty One and coming on the clouds of heaven." (Mt.26:64)

Then the chief priest tore his clothes and said, "He has spoken blasphemy! Why do we need any more witnesses? Look, now you have heard the blasphemy; what do you think?" "He is worthy of death," they answered (Mt.26:65, 66). So they condemned him to death for blasphemy and turned him over to the Roman officials, demanding repeatedly that he be executed. Although Pilate the Roman governor tried to free Jesus, he finally gave in to their demands and had Jesus flogged and handed over to be crucified (Mk.15:15). Thus the dreams and hopes of his disciples came seemingly to an abrupt ending. The religious leaders had accomplished what they thought would put an end to Jesus and the threat he posed to their position and power.

But it was not the end; it was only the hour of darkness before the dawn. Having traced the tragic trajectory of his parables unmistakably to his death, a completely unanticipated turn of events lay quietly in the shadows, waiting patiently to dawn as assuredly as the rising of the sun. The tragedy—his death—turned out to be not the end but the beginning; not a tragedy but a triumph which destroyed the dominance of darkness and ushered in the new age of light—the new age of his resurrection.

Two aspects of the resurrection event stand out in startling contrast: **First**: The lengths to which his enemies went to cover up the reality of the event, and **Second**: The ineptness of Jesus' disciples to accept the undeniable evidence of the event. The fact that these stand in such reverse contrast is one of the most compelling validations of the evidence. His enemies were the first ones to acknowledge the event but tried to hide it; his disciples were the last to acknowledge it but then could not be stopped from broadcasting it—even to the point of giving their lives to proclaim it. As history has borne out, the reality of the resurrection of Jesus has far outlasted the cover-up.

First: *The lengths to which his enemies went to hide it:*

1) They laid plans to prevent a hoax. After Jesus was crucified the Jewish leaders wanted to make sure his disciples did not steal his body and claim that Jesus had in fact risen. They said to Pilate,

> Sir, we remember that while he was still alive that deceiver said, 'After three days I will rise again.' So, give the order for the tomb to be made secure until the third day. Otherwise, his disciples may come and steal the body and tell the people that he has been raised from the dead. (Mt.27:63, 64)

It seems Jesus' enemies were more aware of his talk of resurrection than were his disciples. Evidently Jesus' statements had registered in their consciousness sufficiently to put them on alert. Additionally:

2) There was extensive denial and cover-up so devious it is difficult to fathom. Nowhere is the extent of the intentional rejection of Jesus clearer than in what followed:

> After the Sabbath, at dawn on the first day of the week, Mary Magdalene and the other Mary went to look at the tomb. There was a violent earthquake, for an angel of the Lord came down from heaven and, going to the tomb, rolled back the stone and sat on it. His appearance was like lightning, and his clothes were white as snow. The guards were so afraid of him that they shook and became like dead men... Some of the guards went into the city and reported to the chief priests everything that had happened. (Mt.28:1-11)

> When the chief priests had met with the elders and devised a plan, they gave the soldiers a large sum of money, telling them, "You are to say, 'His disciples came during the night and stole him away while we were asleep.'" If this report gets to the governor, we will satisfy him and keep you out of trouble. So the soldiers took the money and did as they were instructed. And this story has been widely circulated among the Jews to this very day. (28:12-15)

But, though that story was circulated among the Jews for some thirty years (approximately when Matthew wrote his eyewitness account) it seems to have been limited to the Jewish nation. The rumor was extended however beyond Matthew's day by the Council of Jamnia (c.a. A.D. 90). [22]

Second: *The ineptness of the disciples to accept the reality of it:*

This is most evident in their complete failure to grasp Jesus' repeated predictions of it. Those predictions occupied his ministry from beginning to end, finalizing in the actual event itself. He attempted to prepare his disciples by using various language forms: simile, didactic, metaphor, prediction and finally actual presentation of his resurrected body. He appeared bodily to ten of his original Twelve and a week later extended skeptical

---

[22] Encyclopaedia Judaica, "JABNEH": Vol. 9 (New York: The Macmillan Company, 1971), p.1176. See also Encyclopaedia Judaica, Vol. 5 (Jerusalem: Keter Publishing House, 1972), pp. 507-509

Thomas an open invitation to "touch" and "see." He allowed for confusion, rumors, false reports and dejection. He covered every base, opened every door, allowed every latitude of doubt, acknowledged as acceptable both primary and secondary evidence but finally issued the ultimatum: "Stop doubting and believe." (Jn.20:27)

But we're getting ahead of the story—ahead of his many advance notices of his coming resurrection; notices that should have broken through their ineptness. Some of the notices were figurative. The earliest of these (as briefly noted above) is recorded in John's account[23] of the cleansing of the temple. The subsequent conversation between Jesus and the ruling authorities reveals that they hadn't understood his audacious claim.

> When it was almost time for the Jewish Passover, Jesus went up to Jerusalem. In the temple he found men selling cattle, sheep and doves, and others sitting at tables exchanging money. So he made a whip out of cords, and drove all from the temple area, both sheep and cattle; he scattered the coins of the money changers and overturned their tables. To those who sold doves he said, "Get these out of here! How dare you turn my Father's house into a market!" ...Then the Jews demanded of him, "What miraculous sign can you show us to prove you have the authority to do all this?" Jesus answered them, "Destroy this temple, and I will raise it again in three days." (Jn.2:13-19)

His disciples—evidently standing nearby and as astonished as the religious leaders—did not understand at the time that he was referring to his own resurrection, not a rebuilding of the Jerusalem temple. But "after he was raised from the dead, his disciples recalled what he had said. Then they believed the scriptures and the words Jesus had spoken." (v.22)

Jesus also made direct statements to his disciples, but neither did these straightforward words register with them.

---

[23] There is considerable debate over whether John recorded another earlier cleansing of the temple or just inserted at this location (Jn.2:13-19) the one cleansing. Either way, this statement was clearly made, and it surfaced as evidence against Jesus at his trial.

> From that time on Jesus began to explain to his disciples that he must go to Jerusalem and suffer many things at the hands of the elders, chief priests and teachers of the law, and that he must be killed and on the third day be raised to life. (Mt.16:21)

Not that the explanation did any good. Peter, upon hearing that Jesus was going to be killed and raised, took Jesus aside and began to rebuke him (16:22). I suspect Peter didn't even hear the second part of Jesus' statement referring to his resurrection. Six days later, after seeing Jesus transfigured, the three disciples with him were warned, "Don't tell anyone what you have seen, until the Son of Man has been raised from the dead." (17:9) Mark observed earlier that Jesus "spoke plainly about this." (8:32) It still didn't register. Then, the week before his triumphal entry, as they were going up to Jerusalem, he took them aside and told them yet again that he was going to be killed but also raised (Mt.20:17-19).

Jesus arrived in Bethany very likely on the Friday before his triumphal entry into Jerusalem.[24] His friends had prepared a feast in his honor at the home of Simon the Leper (Jn.12:1-12). During the meal, Mary took a flask of expensive perfume and anointed Jesus' head as he was reclining at table. The disciples were indignant at such waste and began to berate Mary. Jesus stepped in and defended her: "Why are you bothering this woman? She has done a beautiful thing to me...When she poured this perfume on my body, she did it to prepare me for burial." (Mt.26:6-12) How much clearer could he have been!? To make sure they understood, he told the Eleven after the last supper, "I'll meet you in Galilee after I have risen." (Mt.26:32) Yet, all these advance notices seem to have passed right over their heads. They simply were incapable of grasping the concept of resurrection!

It was, perhaps, out of deference to their inability to grasp such an unprecedented occurrence that the method Jesus used to reveal it is so interesting. Today as we attempt to grasp that same reality, we are struck by two opposite trails of evidence involved in the revealing of that surreal event: one was probably unavoidable, the other was clearly intentional.

---

[24] op.cit.: Eugene Faulstich, et.al.

1) The unavoidable trail should best be described as "incidental" in that it involved circumstances put in place not by deity but by the enemies of Jesus to make sure no one stole the body. Roman guards standing watch over the tomb just happened to be in the way and were the first involuntary witnesses to whatever it was that happened early that morning. Whatever they saw so shocked the guards they "became like dead men." (Mt.28:4) We are given no medical explanation of what happened to the guards, but obviously a different approach had to be made to Jesus' disciples.

2) The intentional approach Jesus made to his disciples was very unlike the scene involving the Roman guards at the tomb. Rather, it was a gradual and gentle revealing, and it warms the heart to watch Jesus adapt himself to their limited ability to grasp an event so totally outside their experience. And we mustn't be too hard on those original witnesses: nothing like this had ever happened before. But you and I have had 2,000 years to ponder that event—or at least to ponder the possibility of it. How difficult has it been for you and me to get our minds around it? So, let's watch closely as Jesus made his risen self known to his disciples and benefit from it ourselves.

- First: there was simply an empty tomb. Early in the quiet of the morning the door to the new realm of reality was opened ever so slightly.

> On the first day of the week, very early in the morning, the women took the spices they had prepared and went to the tomb. They found the stone rolled away from the tomb, but when they entered, they did not find the body of the Lord Jesus. (Lk.24:1-3)

- Then, a false report was made to Jesus' closest disciples:

> Early on the first day of the week, while it was still dark, Mary Magdalene went to the tomb and saw that the stone had been removed from the entrance. So she came running to Simon Peter and the other disciple...and said, "They have taken the Lord out of the tomb, and we don't know where they have put him." (Jn.20:1,2)

• Peter and John ran to see what Mary was talking about. They entered the empty tomb, saw the grave cloths and reached two different conclusions: John believed (Jn.20:8), and Peter went home confused (Lk.24:12).

• "Mary stood outside the tomb crying."

> As she wept, she bent over to look into the tomb and saw two angels in white, seated where Jesus' body had been, one at the head and the other at the foot. They asked her, "Woman, why are you crying?"

> "They have taken my Lord away," she said, "and I don't know where they have put him." At this, she turned around and saw Jesus standing there, but she did not realize that it was Jesus.

> He asked her, "Woman, why are you crying? Who is it you are looking for?" Thinking he was the gardener, she said, "Sir, if you have carried him away, tell me where you have put him, and I will get him."

> Jesus said to her, "Mary." She turned toward him and cried out in Aramaic, "Rabboni!" (which means "Teacher").

> Jesus said, "Do not hold on to me, for I have not yet ascended to the Father. Go instead to my brothers and tell them, 'I am ascending to my Father and your Father, to my God and your God.'"

> Mary Magdalene went to the disciples with the news: "I have seen the Lord!" And she told them that he had said these things to her. (Jn.20:11-18)

• But the apostles didn't believe the women "because their words seemed to them like nonsense." (Lk.24:2-11) So, even with all these reports coming in and their viewing the empty tomb and seeing the grave cloths, still the event escaped their comprehension.

• There was another occasion toward the close of that same day which showed the gradual process by which Jesus revealed himself to his friends. It is recorded in the 24th chapter of Luke. It reveals seven distinct levels of engagement by which Jesus brought these two disciples to faith. The incident took place on the Road to Emmaus—a little village about 7 miles from Jerusalem. Notice the gentle progression:

Level #1: *Jesus was absent*: Only a man named Cleopas and his companion (perhaps his wife) were on their way home, discussing the events of the past three days (Lk.24:13, 14).

Level #2: *Jesus appeared and joined the two*: "As they talked and discussed these things with each other, Jesus himself came up and walked along with them, but they were kept from recognizing him." (vv.15, 16)

Level #3: *Jesus engaged the two in conversation*: He asked, "What are you discussing together as you walk along?" Quite shocked, Cleopas asked, "Are you only a visitor to Jerusalem and do not know the things that have happened there in these days?" A second question: "What things?" (v.19)

In answer, the two relate the sad and disappointing news of what had happened to Jesus—how their rulers had killed him etc. Dejectedly they confessed, "We had hoped that he was the one who was going to redeem Israel." The two reported also the confusing rumors they had heard about a vision of angels who claimed this Jesus was alive (vv. 19-24).

Level #4: *Jesus began to instruct them from the Scriptures*:

> How foolish you are, and how slow of heart to believe all that the prophets have spoken. Did not the Christ have to suffer these things and then to enter his glory? And beginning with Moses and all the prophets, he explained to them what was said in all the Scriptures concerning himself. (Lk.24:25, 26)

Level #5: *Jesus drew them into action*:

> As they approached the village to which they were going, Jesus acted as if he were going farther. But they urged him strongly, 'Stay with us, for it is nearly evening; the day is almost over.' So he went in to stay with them. (Lk.24:28, 29)

Level #6: *Jesus sat at table to eat with them*. "When he was at table with them, he took bread, broke it and began to give it to them." (v. 30)

Level #7: *Jesus revealed himself to them.* "Then their eyes were opened and they recognized him, and he disappeared from their sight." (v.31) Cleopas and his companion immediately rushed back to Jerusalem, ran up the stairs to the upper room and, while trying to catch their breath, they heard the confirming report that Jesus had indeed been raised and had appeared to Simon. They then gave their report of all that had happened on the road and how Jesus had revealed himself to them as he broke the bread (vv.33-35). While they were still talking, Jesus himself stood among them and said, "Peace be with you." (v.36) Still, the resurrected Christ was difficult to grasp. "They were startled and frightened, thinking they saw a ghost." (v.37)

He said to them:

> Why are you troubled, and why do doubts rise in your minds? Look at my hands and my feet. It is I myself! Touch me and see; a ghost does not have flesh and bones as you see I have. (vv.38, 39)

> When he had said this, he showed them his hands and feet. And while they still did not believe it because of joy and amazement, he asked them, 'Do you have anything here to eat?' They gave him a piece of broiled fish, and he took it and ate it in their presence. (vv.40-43)

Picking up the record of that same event in John's account, we are given further information. For some unknown reason Thomas was not with the other disciples in the upper room that night.

> Now Thomas (called Didymus), one of the Twelve, was not with the disciples when Jesus came. So the other disciples told him, "We have seen the Lord." But he said to them, "Unless I see the nail marks in his hands and put my finger where the nails were, and put my hand into his side, I will not believe it." (Jn.20:24, 25)

Here's an example of the two kinds of evidence (primary and secondary) which are essential to unreserved belief in the resurrection and to the ongoing spread of that faith down through the centuries to this present day. The disciples who were in the upper room that first night Jesus appeared were given *primary* evidence when Jesus presented himself to them in bodily form (Jn.20:19, 20). Thomas was absent (20:24). When the others told him what *they* had seen, it was not sufficient for Thomas, and he told them so in no uncertain terms: "Unless I see the nail marks in his hand and put my finger where the nails were, and put my hand in his side, I will not believe it."

> A week later his disciples were in the house again, and Thomas was with them. Though the doors were locked, Jesus came and stood among them and said, "Peace be with you." Then he said to Thomas, "Put your finger here; see my hands. Reach out your hand and put it into my side. Stop doubting and believe." (Jn.20:26,27)

Thomas confessed in astonishment: "My Lord and my God!" (v.28)

Thomas thus joined that band of people of whom Thomas Yancey observed:

> Jesus, if one may use such language, 'broke his own rules' about faith. He made his identity so obvious that no disciple could ever deny him again (and none did). In a word, Jesus overwhelmed the witnesses' faith: anyone who saw the resurrected Jesus lost the freedom of choice to believe or disbelieve. Jesus was now irrefutable.[25]

But only a few experienced such intimate interface with the risen Christ. What about the rest of us? Jesus also recognized all those who could not be eyewitnesses. He acknowledged the difference between primary and secondary evidence and actually placed a unique blessing on those who come to faith through secondary evidence: After saying to Thomas, "Because you have seen me, you have believed;" he then added, "Blessed are those who have not seen and yet believe." (v.29) So, we who come later are blessed

---

[25] Phillip Yancey, *The Jesus I Never Knew* (Grand Rapids: Zondervan, 1949), p.216.

as we come to faith. Years later Peter wrote to those believers scattered throughout the Mediterranean world:

> Though you have not seen him, you love him; and even though you do not see him now, you believe in him and are filled with an inexpressible and glorious joy, for you are receiving the goal of your faith, the salvation of your souls. (1Pet.1:8,9)

Why is this important for us? Because, all the rest of us must come to faith through the door of secondary evidence. There are no eyewitnesses of the resurrection today. But adequate evidence of the resurrection is available today; he hasn't left us as orphans. He was raised and is coming back!

> Do not let your hearts be troubled. You believe in God, believe also in me. My Father's house has many rooms; if that were not so, would I have told you that I am going there to prepare a place for you? And if I go and prepare a place for you, I will come back and take you with me that you also may be where I am. (John 4:1-3)

So, if you are still struggling whether or not to believe, don't give up; coming to faith is at the same time both a thrilling search and a disturbing journey because we are being called to accept the totally *unexpected*. Fortunately, in Jesus we are being called not only to accept the *unexpected* but also are forced to acknowledge the *unexcelled*. And nothing less than the *unexpected* could have produced the *unexcelled*. Check it out; there is no ethic which excels what Jesus taught or any reward that exceeds what Jesus offered. The totally unequaled nobility of his call validates the absolute uniqueness of his claim.

And make no mistake about it, his claim is clear. After he was raised ...

> ... Jesus came to them and said, "All authority in heaven and on earth has been given to me. Therefore go and make disciples of all nations, baptizing them in the name of the Father and of the Son and of the Holy Spirit, and teaching them to obey everything I have commanded you. And surely I am with you always, to the very end of the age." (Mt.28:18-20)

Chapter 20

CONCLUSION

I N THE PREFACE to this work we made an admission as we attempted to combine the Beatitudes and the Parables into a single volume: *"... the birth process is even more stressful if you have twins—which is what this book is—two creations wrapped in one cover; related and perhaps even strangely Siamese: joined at the head and heart. Hopefully the two parts will beat with one life and where the one goes so will go the other. If the reader is blessed by the one, the reader will be blessed by the other."*

Did we achieve our objective? Is there a literary license as well as a theological theme that would allow connecting the Beatitudes and the Parables — parables in general and the Grace Parables in particular? Perhaps by using a modern metaphor we can establish a legitimate correlation between the two:

The Beatitudes are concentrated principles; axioms or propositions which state eternal truths so fundamental to understanding the nature of God's kingdom that they serve as underpinnings of that kingdom. They are abbreviated—giving them simplicity. Yet, at the same time, they are enigmatic enough to engage the mind and heart for years of study and meditation. One can plumb the depths and explore the heights of the Beatitudes only to find there is no boundary which can be assigned these great truths.

The Beatitudes are similar to today's texting via Twitter—short, encrypted messages which require study and, perhaps, even knowledge of the culture to decipher: FYI, LOL, BTW, SYS etc. Thus, embedded in the Beatitudes (those coded abbreviations of divine wisdom) is information relevant to the subject at hand: God's reign in your life.

Parables, on the other hand, are more like blogging. Or better yet, like a video sent over YouTube; fully fleshed out in 3-D and living color, containing all the details necessary for a full understanding of the message. Parables paint pictures on the mind and leave impressions on the heart. Parables are not ultimately for information, but for transformation. They have the power not only to convey facts but to convict hearts. *Parables are the melodies that carry the lyrics of the kingdom into the heart of those who have ears to hear.*

But something was lacking in my original draft of the Beatitudes and the Parables. The study seemed incomplete. A piece of the puzzle was missing. All the work I had put into writing this book suddenly seemed truncated; like an unfinished sentence. As I stated in the Preface, it was like standing in a forest but unable to see the forest for the trees.

Finally, I saw the forest: *the Resurrection of Jesus is the forest.* The references Jesus made prior to it, the event itself, and then all that the eyewitnesses said about it in the years that followed—yes, and for which they gave their lives attest to its validity. The Resurrection is the center and the circumference—the wrapping that binds it all together; the event to which all else points. It is the missing piece of the puzzle—not just the puzzle in my mind over this book but *the* missing piece of the puzzle of life itself. Having now seen that missing piece, we come to the close of our study with a sense of completeness.

May the reality of the resurrected Jesus so deeply touch your heart that you can say with confidence:

Before the throne of God above, I have a strong and perfect plea.
A great High Priest whose name is Love who ever lives and pleads for me.
My name is graven on his hands, my name is written on his heart.
I know that while in heaven he stands, no tongue can bid me thence depart.

When Satan tempts me to despair and tells me of the guilt within.
Upward I look and see him there who made an end of all my sin.
Because the sinless Savior died my sinful soul is counted free;
For God the Just is satisfied to look on him and pardon me.

Behold him there the Risen Lamb my perfect spotless righteousness.
The great unchangeable I Am, the King of glory and of grace.
One with himself I cannot die, my soul is purchased by his blood.
My life is hid with Christ on high, with Christ my Savior and my God.[26]

Charitie Lees Smith

---

[26] Charitie Lees Smith, "Before the Throne of God Above." Charitie published her poetry in leaflet form as early as 1860, and a number of her collected works were eventually published as *Within the Veil* in 1867. "Before the Throne" was written in 1863 under the title "The Advocate."

Bibliography

Baron, Salo Wittmayer. *A Social and Religious History of the Jews.* New York: Columbia Univ. Press, 1952.

Chambers, Oswald. *My Utmost For His Highest.* New York: Dodd, Mead & Company, 1935.

Encyclopaedia Judaica, New York: The Macmillan Company, 1971.

Encyclopaedia Judaica, London: Keter Publishing Jerusalem Ltd. 1972.

Eubanks, Dan. *Unresolved Guilt in the Church.* Austin, TX: Firm Foundation, 1997.

Francis, Dr. James Allan. *The Real Jesus and Other Sermons.* Philadelphia: Judson Press. 1926.

Faulstich, Eugene & Rood, Michael J. "What Time Is It?," *1999 Chronology Books.* Two Harbors, MN, New Moon Publishers, 1999.

Geisler, Norman. "The Collapse of Modern Atheism," *The Intellectuals Speak Out About God.* Regnery Gateway, Inc., 1984.

Howell, W. C. and Fleishman, E. A. (eds.), *Human Performance and Productivity. Vol .2: Information Processing and Decision Making.* Hillsdale, NJ: Erlbaum, 1982.

Lewis, C. S. *Surprised By Joy.* London: Geofrey Bles, 1955.

Nouwen, Henri. *The Return of the Prodigal Son.* New York: Doubleday, 1994.

Schonfield, Hugh J. *The Passover Plot.* New York: Bernard Geis Assoc., 1965.

Shakespeare, William. *Hamlet*, Act 1, scene 3.

Smith, Charitie Lees. *Before the Throne of God Above.* Collected works Published as *Within the Veil*, 1867.

Wells, H. G. quoted by N. B. Hardeman in the Dallas Lectures, (Dallas, TX, Eugene Smith Publisher, 1943), pp.122-125.

Woodroof, Horace M., *Stone Wall College.* Nashville, TN: Aurora Publishers, 1970.

Woodroof, Tim, *Walk This Way.* Colorado Springs: NavPress, 1999.

Yancey, Phillip, *The Jesus I Never Knew.* Grand Rapids: Zondervan, 1949.

Acknowledgments

Sayings That Saved My Sanity first appeared under the title *Famous Sayings of Jesus*. The new title is due primarily to an unbelievable chain of events involving several key individuals. Special acknowledgment is due Terry Smith who, at the very time he was involved in publishing his own journey from darkness to light (the book ***Delta Blues***), took the interest and the time to encourage me to write this book. He has served also in opening doors to a wider readership, both on college campuses and now in the area of those incarcerated in prisons, as well as those bound by their own self-made (or others-made) prisons of troubled mind and confused direction.

Others involved in that chain of events include Nathan Lee, a Nashville musician and founder of a non-profit ministry "*Send Musicians To Prison*." He was so impressed with the first edition of this book that he gave a copy to Curt Campbell, director of "Men of Valor," another non-profit work dedicated to providing hope to prisoners. Curt introduced the book to the prison in Nashville and arranged for classes to be taught using the book as the study material.

Also, Mr. Blair J. Leibach, warden of the Metro-Davidson County Detention Facility (Nashville Tennessee) is due our appreciation for allowing those classes to be taught and for the musical concert which came as a result. The whole chain of events could not have happened without his helpful assistance.

Finally, two others whose stories appear in the front fly leaf must be given special recognition: Gino and Erin Greganti, whose story warms the heart of everyone who reads it. Many thanks to them for sharing their life struggle with us. Gino also designed the cover for this second edition.

A fuller account of this chain of events and those involved in it can be found in the Foreword.

A special word of thanks to F. LaGard Smith for very crucial editing in the early stages of this effort.

Also, to those who contributed financially to this publication and to those who wrote endorsements; to Maxine Carroll who worked so faithfully as proof-reader, to graphic artists Scot Harris, Jane Gibson and Brent Alexander of Gospel Light Publishing Co., I express my appreciation.

James S. Woodroof
December. 2014